THE

FOOTMAN'S DIRECTORY,

AND

Butler's Remembrancer;

OR, THE

Advice of Onesimus to his young Friends:

COMPRISING,

HINTS ON THE ARRANGEMENT AND PERFORMANCE OF THEIR WORK;

RULES FOR SETTING OUT TABLES AND SIDEBOARDS;

THE ART OF WAITING AT TABLE,
AND CONDUCTING LARGE AND SMALL PARTIES;

DIRECTIONS FOR CLEANING PLATE, GLASS, FURNITURE,
CLOTHES, AND ALL OTHER THINGS WHICH COME
WITHIN THE CARE OF A MAN-SERVANT;

AND

ADVICE RESPECTING BEHAVIOUR TO SUPERIORS, TRADESPEOPLE,
AND FELLOW-SERVANTS.

With an APPENDIX, comprising various useful Receipts and Tables.

LONDON:

PRINTED FOR THE AUTHOR;
AND SOLD BY J. HATCHARD AND SON,
187, PICCADILLY.

1823.

PRYOR PUBLICATIONS
WHITSTABLE AND WALSALL

Specialist in Facsimile Reproductions

MEMBER OF
INDEPENDENT PUBLISHERS GUILD

75 Dargate Road, Yorkletts, Whitstable,
Kent CT5 3AE, England.
Tel. & Fax: (01227) 274655

Email: alan@pryor-publish.clara.net

http://home.clara.net/pryor-publish

Kent Exporter of the Year Awards Winner 1998

ISBN 0 946014 70 1

A full list of Titles sent free on request.

First Published 1823

Printed by
Hillman Printers
(Frome) Ltd.
Handlemaker Road,
Marston Trading Estate,
Frome, Somerset BA11 4RW.
Tel: 01373 473526 Fax: 01373 451852

LETTER

TO

THE PUBLISHER.

———————

HONOURED SIR,

   I HOPE you will excuse the liberty I take in writing to you; but having written a few directions and observations for the use of Gentlemen's Servants, I was advised, after letting some of my friends see them, to ask you if you thought they might be made useful if published My endeavour has been to promote the comfort of those whom I have had the honour to serve, and to benefit my fellow-servants. Having been often employed myself in instructing young persons who had never been out in service before, I imagined that a set of rules regularly laid down for the use of domestic servants might be very acceptable, and save a great deal of trouble to such ladies and gentlemen as only keep one footman, and are therefore obliged, if they happen to engage one who is ignorant, either to instruct him themselves, or to part with him, even when he may be likely to suit them very well in the course of a little time. I thought, likewise, that it would be very useful to servants who, coming from the country, may not have had an opportunity of improving themselves as they might have done in town. I have endeavoured to direct those for whose service I have written, not only in their business, but their conduct and principles, and have given them scriptural examples respecting their duties, and the practice of all that is required of them. If you, Sir, approve the design of my work, and will condescend to become the publisher of it, I hope that any defects in its style and execution will be kindly overlooked by the public, under the consideration that it is the production of one who has not had any of the advantages of education, but who is earnestly desirous of doing all the good that may come within his power.

I am, honoured Sir,

Your most obedient and humble Servant,

ONESIMUS.

CONTENTS.

APPENDIX.

APPENDIX.

CONTENTS.

ERRATA.

Page 110, line 4, *for* the table mats may, *read*, the tables may.

—— 142, —— 5 from bottom, *for*, Let two or three glasses be put for each of the company, as they in general help themselves, *read*, Let two or three glasses be put to each decanter, as in general the company serve themselves.

THE

FOOTMAN'S DIRECTORY,

&c.

I ENTREAT you, my young friends, duly to consider the directions and observations which I have set forth in the following pages for your benefit; and which are intended not only for those who may be already in comfortable situations, but also for young men who may be desirous of earning their bread by honest service, and yet are entirely ignorant of the duties which they will in that case be expected to perform. An earnest wish to serve all such as much as is in my power, has induced me to publish the fruits of my own experience as a domestic servant; and if it be received with the same desire to be benefited by it that the author had of doing good in writing it, I trust that, with the blessing of God, all who read it may be instructed by it, and that he will give them grace and wisdom to do the things which are right and just in his sight.

Such of my readers as may be now candidates for gentlemen's service, must consider, that it is a way of life wholly different from any that they have been accustomed to ; comprising comforts, privileges, and pleasures, which are to be met with in but few other situations; and, on the other hand, difficulties, trials of temper, and self-denials, beyond what you might be called on to bear in some other state of life. When you go into service, all the ways in which you may have been indulged at home must be given up ; and you will find it equally to your comfort and profit to have none but those of your employers, as far as they may be consistent with justice and moral government. Reflect that when you once engage yourself in a situation, neither your time nor your abilities are any longer your own, but your employers', and they have consequently a claim on them whenever they may be required.

Some persons speak of servants as if they were so much beneath them as to be unworthy of notice; but this adds nothing to their own respectability, and only betrays their ignorance and pride. There is no degradation in being a menial, except you fail in the duties of one ; no disgrace in wearing a livery, unless you bring reproach on it by your behaviour. I have never been ashamed of being in livery but when I have seen other servants disgrace it. The various stations in life are appointed by God ; all are useful and honourable in their different degrees. We find from history and Holy Writ, that domestic servants have frequently been intrusted with matters of the utmost importance to their employers; and the God of heaven and earth has condescended to take notice of them and bless them, and bless their masters and mistresses for their sakes. Of this we have a memorable instance in Joseph, who was sold by his brethren to the Ishmaelites, and bought of them by Potiphar to be his domestic servant. In this capacity Joseph acquitted himself with integrity and uprightness. " And his master saw that the Lord was with him, and that the Lord made all that he did to prosper by his hand. *The Lord blessed the Egyptian's house for Joseph's sake;* and the blessing of the Lord was upon all that he had in the house and in the field. And he left all that he had in Joseph's hand; and he knew not ought he had, save the bread which he did eat."—Genesis, chap. xxxix.

Have we not here a most delightful and encouraging instance of a domestic servant's enjoying the special favour of God and the unlimited confidence of his master? but remember, my young friends, that Joseph walked in the ways of the Lord. Hear what he says in his answer to Potiphar's adulterous wife, when tempted to rob his master and sin against God. " Behold, my master wotteth not what is with me in the house, and he hath committed all that he hath to my hand. There is none greater in this house than I; neither hath he kept back any thing from me but thee, because thou art his wife:

how then can I do this great wickedness, and sin against God ?"

O my young friends, may this noble and God-fearing answer be lastingly impressed upon our minds, and be ever found in our mouths when we are tempted to act unjustly or to go astray. The Scriptures abound in pleasing and encouraging instances of servants faithfully performing their duties, and the favour of God and the confidence of their masters rewarding their labours; and I might mention the fidelity of Mordecai, who in his capacity of porter to King Ahasuerus, saved that monarch from the violent hands of his two chamberlains; and the mutual kindness and attachment between the prophet Elisha and his servant : not the servant Gehazi, who, when his master had miraculously cured Naaman, the captain of the host of the King of Syria, of his leprosy, without the desire of reward, ran after him to extort money from him for himself; in which dishonest conduct he is daily imitated by too many servants who live with medical gentlemen that are willing to give their advice to the poor gratis, but whose good intentions are often frustrated by the avarice of their servants, who will not let the poor see their masters until they have wrung something out of them for the privilege. Let such persons remember the punishment of Gehazi; the disorder of which the prophet had cured Naaman cleaved to himself, and he went out from his master's presence " a leper white as snow."

Happy are the families where servants study the comfort and welfare of their employers, who in return do the same by them. The kind admonition of an affectionate master or mistress is always to be listened to with respect; for, the Wise Man saith, " as an earring of gold, and an ornament of fine gold, so is a wise reproof upon an obedient ear."— Prov. xxiv. 12.

It may be your lot to find a master or mistress who may act unkindly and unjustly towards you, as Laban did to Jacob his servant and son-in-law; but if you do your duty, you will be more happy in your integrity than your employers can be in their injustice. . I would rather be the oppressed than stand in the place of the oppressor. Patience is ever acceptable to God, and in due time will be rewarded, because God hath promised that it shall be so; and when have his promises failed? Jacob's master shifted and shuffled him about for twenty years, and changed his wages ten times; yet the Lord blessed the upright and honest servant, because he had done that which was just between his master and himself.

Let these considerations, my young friends, stimulate you to truth and faithfulness in your situations through life. You will find in the class of society with which you are about to associate, some of the most profligate of people; that is, in a refined way, if I may be allowed the expression : also some of the most proud and ignorant, glorying in their insolence and profaneness. Happily they are not all so. I know a great number who are held in just esteem, and have been honourably rewarded for their fidelity and good conduct; and I trust, for your own sakes, you will make intimate companions of none other than persons of this description. You must always bear in mind that your character is your bread and your all; you must therefore watch over it incessantly, to keep it unstained and undeniable, as without this it is useless to seek after any respectable service whatsoever. Nor can we wonder at the scrupulousness of ladies and gentlemen in this particular, or at the minute inquiries they make into every point of a stranger's character, before they are willing to admit him in the capacity of a servant beneath their roof; as, from the moment they do it, he becomes of necessity intrusted, to a certain degree, with their property, and even their lives: and how many sad instances are there, of which we have all heard, of masters being robbed by dishonest servants, and even their lives being exposed to danger through evil connexions, formed unknown to them by the inmates of their family! Remember also, that it is not sufficient that your own conduct be good, if you associate with those whose conduct is bad: you will be judged by them at least as much as by yourself. St. Paul observes, that " evil communications corrupt good manners;" and how forcibly does the Psalmist say, " Blessed is the man that walketh not in the counsel of the ungodly, nor standeth in the way of sinners, nor sitteth in the seat of the scornful."

If it should please the Lord to promote and prosper your fidelity and industry, show your gratitude by increased exertions for your employers, and kindness and consideration for all around you. If your place should prove lucrative, be mindful of your poor parents, who may be getting into years, and recollect how often they may have pinched themselves that you might be fed; and forget not any of your relations that may be in need : neither forget your own old age, which must come, and may find you both poor and helpless, unless you lay up, in the time of prosperity, something for the time of need. Nor is this careful foresight at all at variance with a grateful and cheerful enjoyment of all the blessings that lawfully come within our reach. Solomon himself says, " There is nothing better for a man than that he should eat and drink, and that he should make his soul enjoy good in his labour ; " and also, that " every man should eat and drink, and enjoy the good of all his labour—*it is the gift of God.*"

Truly blessed, my young friends, are those who have the blessing of God on their labour ; for this alone maketh rich, and causeth no sorrow. Better is it to be of a humble spirit with the lowly, than to divide the spoil with the proud. " He that is slow to anger is better than the mighty, and he that ruleth his spirit than he that taketh a city."

Remember what the Wise Man hath said in another place: " The beginning of strife is as when one letteth out water." Leave off contention, therefore: before it be meddled with, put a bridle on your tongue, and a guard on your lips, that you be not hasty in expression, for in the multitude of words there is sin. If you feel the want of wisdom to direct you in your conduct through life, ask it in humble prayer of the Lord, who giveth liberally and upbraideth not.

And now, my dear young friends, I again entreat your attention to the following pages, in which I have laid down such rules for the convenient performance of your work, and the fulfilment of your duties, as from my own experience I have reason to think you will find useful. Not that I mean to propose them as a fixed standard; for, after all, the duty of a servant is to do things in that way which his master may like best; but as a general guide, and affording an insight into matters connected with gentlemen's service. I have found the methods I have prescribed in the ensuing pages very satisfactory to those whom I have had the honour to serve; and some of the friends I am now addressing can bear witness to the manner in which I have always endeavoured to acquit myself of the duties that have fallen to my lot, and the kindness and consideration with which I have been treated in consequence by many families, both during the time I lived with them, and after I had quitted their service. I have had many afflictions and many trials; but I have endeavoured to view them all as appointed by God, and sanctified to my good: accordingly he has supported me, and raised me up kind friends, under them, and bountifully provided for me through his providence. I am now about to retire from my avocations as a domestic servant; and in thus addressing myself to all those of my own rank and pursuits in life, I would have them consider me as taking an affectionate farewell of them, and imagine me as giving them in person the friendly counsels and directions which for their sakes have flowed from my pen. Be ye therefore, my friends, watchful, careful, and honest, in all your dealings. Beware of bad company and of drunkenness. War, famine, disease, and accident, daily slay thousands of the human race; but drunkenness and its consequences destroy tens of thousands. . Behold the family of a drunken man! What poverty, what distress, what sorrow, are scattered over it! Shun, above all, the haunts of lewd women, and remember how forcibly we are warned of their snares in Holy Writ. " Let not thine heart incline to her ways; go not astray in her paths: for she hath cast down many wounded ; yea, many strong men have been slain by her. Her house is the way to hell, going down to the chambers of death."—Prov. ix. 25—27.

Many, very many, my young friends, have I known, whose prospects in life, and all their en-

joyments, have been early blasted by not attending
to warnings like these, who have gone about like
vagabonds, diseased in body, dispirited in mind,
outcasts from all the most respectable part of society, and a burden to themselves. May the God
of all good keep us from every temptation to such hei-
nous and overwhelming sins ; and as it is to be feared
that the young and thoughtless often fall into them
from having too much idle time, which they know
not how to employ, let me exhort you, my friends,
to devote your evenings, or whatever leisure mo-
ments may fall to your share, to the Bible and de-
votional tracts, books of travels or history, lives
of good men, and accounts of any thing useful or
ingenious; to make extracts from them into a clean
paper book, which will greatly improve both your
writing and your memory; to practise accounts ;
and, in short, to improve yourselves by every means
in your power. You will thus not only be better
enabled to fulfil the duties of your situation, and to
express your gratitude to God for the blessings of
it ; but you will be fit for any other, should you
ever wish to leave service, and to settle in some re-
putable manner, so as to maintain a family respect-
ably, and show yourselves as kind in your own way
as masters over others, as you may have found, or
wished to find, those who were for an allotted period master over you. With an earnest prayer,
that it may please God, in his infinite mercy, to
bless us all in the several stations which in his wis-

dom he hath appointed us to fill, and to give us grace to perform the respective duties belonging to each with cheerfulness and devout submission to his holy will, I conclude my general exhortation for your welfare, and enter on the particular statements connected more immediately with your domestic duties.

EARLY RISING.

In order for a servant to get through his work well, he should do it at proper times and in proper order, and should likewise be properly dressed for each separate department of it. The first requisite, my friends, for all this is EARLY RISING; by which means you secure an opportunity, before the family is up, of doing the dirtiest part of your work without being liable to interruption. This you will find an unspeakable comfort, as nothing is more disagreeable than to be called off in the midst of it, and forced to run about with dirty hands and dirty clothes, which must inevitably be the case if you defer this part of your work until every body is stirring and bustling about. Hence you will always find an hour before the family is up, more profitable for business than two hours afterwards. It is highly necessary to have a dress on purpose for the dirtiest part of your work, and never to do it in the clothes or livery in which you have to wait on the family; as it can scarcely be imagined that the dress in which we clean boots, shoes, knives and forks, and lamps, can be proper afterwards to attend ladies and gentlemen in. I am sorry to say, however, that many families will not allow their servants things proper for such occasions; and then are unjust enough to find fault with them if they appear dirty: but how do they think it possible for a servant to look clean, who has only one suit to do his work in, and to appear in, before company? There is no class of persons to whom cleanliness of person and attire is of more consequence, than to servants in genteel families. I have known several obliged to leave their places solely from negligence in this respect; and I myself have, from a sense of its importance, refused places where a proper working dress has been refused me; deeming it equally disgraceful to a servant and his master, to be obliged to appear in dirty clothes at a time of day when all his dirty work ought to be over. Before going to a new place, therefore, be very particular in stating what you may require, and understanding what you are to have, as no servant ought to take a situation without ascertaining, as nearly as possible, that it is likely to suit him and he to suit it; otherwise he only involves a lady or gentleman in unnecessary trouble and expense, and risks injuring his own character, by appearing to run about from one place to another. You will generally find that large families give the most clothes to servants, whilst those who keep only one or two, at most, give the fewest, though in fact they ought to give the most, as the servant has of course more work to do in proportion. Whether a family be large or small, however, ought not to be any consideration, as every servant should have a sufficiency of clothes to appear neat and respectable in, both for his own sake and the sake of those whom he may serve. A pair of overalls, with a proper waistcoat and jacket, and a leather apron, is the best dress for dirty work; but if you have to attend on a gentleman, you must have white linen aprons for the purpose.

Having pointed out the dress proper for your work, I shall proceed to give some directions respecting the manner of performing it; and though you may not be able to do it *exactly* in the order I shall lay down, yet I would by all means have you follow it as *nearly* as you can; for, without proper *order*, you will always find yourself in a state of hurry and confusion. I know that a great deal must depend on the habits of the family you live with, the number of servants that may be kept, and whether you have much or little to do. In any case, however, you ought to do all that you can of your work, especially of the dirtiest part of it, before the family be up. If, however, they rise before you can get it finished, then do first that which they are most likely to want by the time they are up; of which you must judge for yourself, as the habits of fa-

milies differ so much, that it is impossible to lay
down any particular rules which will apply to all.
We will begin, however, with

BOOTS AND SHOES,

As being things sometimes required in a hurry,
and which ought, therefore, always to be kept in
readiness.   For the operation of cleaning boots and
shoes, good brushes and good blacking are imple-
ments indispensably necessary, without which no
credit will be gained by the operator, whatever
labour he may lavish on his work.   In the first
place remove all the loose dirt with a wooden knife,
which you can make yourself, and never use a
sharp steel knife for the purpose, as by doing so
the leather is too often cut, and the boots and shoes
spoiled before you are aware of it.   When you
have scraped off all the dirt that you can with
the knife, take the hard brush and brush off the
remainder and all the dust, which you must be
particular in doing, or you will not get them to
look well; they must also be quite dry before you
black them, or else they will not shine.   Do not
put on too much blacking at a time, for, if it
dries into the leather before you can use the shining
brush, the leather will look brown instead of black.
If you have boot-trees, never clean either your boots
or shoes without them, as they look far better by

4

being done upon them; but take care that the trees themselves are always kept clean and free from dust, that they may not dirty the inside of the boots or shoes; for the same reason never put one shoe within another, and when you clean boots or shoes belonging to the ladies, be careful that your hands are clean, in order that the linings may not get soiled. Some of these are done with milk, or particular mixtures, and only a little blacking used for the edges of the soles: it should be put on with a small piece of sponge, so as not to dirty the upper leathers, upon which the proper mixtures may be put with another piece of sponge or a little flannel. Always stir your blacking up well before you use it, put it on the brush with a piece of sponge tied to the end of a small cane, and keep it corked when you have done with it, as it gets spoiled by being exposed to the air. If your boots and shoes do not look bright after once blacking and rubbing, do them again until you are satisfied with them, and when finished, always put them immediately away into the places proper for them, that they may be kept clean and in readiness. It is the best, if you have time, always to scrape off the dirt when *wet* from boots or shoes; but never place them near the fire to dry, as that cracks the leather; it ought always to be done very gradually. There are various ways of cleaning boot-tops, which are regulated in a great measure by what the fashion may happen to be, or what colour a gentleman may prefer. In all cases, however, the tops are done the last; great care therefore is necessary that the bottoms do not get dirtied whilst the tops are doing. To prevent this, take a piece of paper, or of parchment, which is much better, and cover the top part of the boot whilst the leg of it is cleaning, and afterwards cover the leg part whilst the top is cleaning. If it be meant to be of a light colour, the top requires to be made pretty wet, but not more so than is absolutely necessary, as the copperas used in the mixture is apt to penetrate through the leather, particularly if the boots are put near the fire to dry them quickly; this ought therefore always to be avoided. It is much better to let them dry gradually in the sun, or at least at a distance from the fire. You will find it necessary to oil or grease leather boots and shoes to keep them from cracking and render them supple, otherwise they will not wear well; but you should never put on oil alone, particularly in hot weather, as it will soak through the pores of the leather when the leg gets warm, and by that means take off the polish from the boots, and make the stockings dirty and uncomfortable. Directions for mixtures proper for this purpose, as also for rendering leather water-proof, and for making blacking, will be found in the Appendix. I therefore will now proceed to the next branch of work which it is advisable to get out of the way as early in the day as possible, and that is

CLEANING KNIVES AND FORKS.

To do these properly, you must have a smooth
board, free from knots, or, what is much better,
covered with leather; as that both polishes the
knives and keeps them from notches, which entirely spoil the cutting and the look of knives, and
cannot be prevented if the board upon which they
may be cleaned should be worn rough and uneven
at the edge. Every servant ought to see that he
has proper utensils and tools to do his work with;
and not to spoil and ruin good things, for want of
asking for what is proper. The cost of a convenient knife-board is a mere trifle, but the cost of
a good set of knives and forks is a subject of serious
expense. Some families are unwilling to allow their
servants proper things when asked for; but some
servants, on the other hand, are so careless, or so
lazy, that rather than ask for what they ought to
have, they will go on making any shift, and spoil-
ing as many things as would pay for all they want
ten times over; which is a great injustice to their
employers, as they cannot always know what is
wanting or worn out, unless told by the servant,
under whose notice such things come every day,
and often many times in the day. Let me exhort
you then, my young friends, always to treat the
property of your master and mistress with as much

care as if it was your own, and to inform them immediately, on all occasions, of any thing that may be likely to injure or endanger it. If your knife-board be covered with leather, melt a sufficient quantity of mutton suet, and put it hot upon the leather with a piece of flannel; then take two pieces of soft Bath brick, and rub them one against the other over the leather till it is covered with the powder, which rub in until no grease comes through when a knife is passed over the leather, which you will easily know by the knife keeping its polish bright and clean. If you have only a plain board, it will be enough to rub the Bath brick two or three times over it; for, if you put on too much at once, it will make the blades of your knives look rough and scratched. Let your board be neither too high nor too low, but of a proper height, so that you may move your hands and arms backward and forward with ease to yourself; it should be also so set as that you may be a little on the stoop while cleaning your knives. Take a knife in each hand, holding them back to back; stand opposite the middle of the board, lay your knives flat upon it, and do not bear too hard upon them when you expand your arms, only just enough so to feel the board; bear rather harder in drawing your hands together, taking care, however, to keep the knives *flat* on the board; by this means you will find it easier to clean two knives at a time than only one, and you will be less liable to break them, as good knives being made of the best steel, will snap when pressed on too heavily; moreover, a knife that is lightly cleaned, has a better polish than one which is pressed on hardly, and it is of course much more easily done. Many will say that they cannot clean two knives at once; or that they can get through them faster one by one : but I can assure them from my own experience, that if they will only try it a few times in the way I recommend, they will find it not only much more expeditious, but much easier likewise. Be particular in keeping a good edge on your knives. It is very disagreeable to see a lady or gentleman carving with a knife so blunt that it will scarcely cut; it is provoking to them, and disgraceful to the servant, whose duty it is to have his knives and forks in proper order, and who has the mortification, as he stands by, to see the dissatisfaction his neglect occasions. Carving-knives in particular ought to be kept sharp, which may easily be done by taking one in each hand, back to back, when cleaning, scarcely letting them touch the board when you expand your arms, but when drawing your hands together again, bearing a little hard on the edges of the knives; this will give them both a good edge and a fine polish, and is much better than sharpening them, as some do, with a steel, or blue whetstone, which gives them a scratched appearance. Servants are often blamed because the points of the knives are worn out before the other part ; but it is not their fault ; for, the points being most used, of course require the most cleaning, which causes them to grow thin, both at the back part as well as the edge. Nor is it always a servant's fault that the knives are notched; the carver is often the occasion of it, by not hitting the joints well, but wrenching them apart with the knife, and trying to do that by *force*, which ought to be done only by *skill*. A good set of knives is however soon spoiled if neglected by a servant, and as they are not only very expensive, but likewise things that are always narrowly looked at upon a table, they ought always to be particularly attended to. The best way to clean steel forks is to fill a small oyster-barrel, or something of that kind, with fine gravel, brickdust, or sand, mixed with a little hay or moss; make it moderately damp, press it well down, and let it always be kept damp. By running the prongs of the steel forks a few times into this, all the stains on them will be removed; then have a small thin stick shaped like a knife, with a leather round it, to polish between the prongs, and also the other parts, having first carefully brushed off the dust from them as soon as you have taken them out of the tub. It often happens that a knife-board is spoiled by cleaning forks upon it, and likewise the backs of the knives: by putting the points of the forks on the board while polishing them, they are apt to stick in, and bring pieces out; and by cleaning the backs of the knives on the edges of the board, notches are made in it which afterwards notch the edges of the knives when cleaning. To prevent

this, have a piece of *old hat,* or leather, to put on
the part of the board where you clean your forks
and the backs of your knives. When you have
done one side of a pair of knives, change them ;
that is, put that which you had in your right hand
into your left, still taking care to keep them back to
back ; by this means there will be no danger of
striking the edges against each other. After they
are cleaned you must have a dry linen cloth to take
the dust off the blades, and a damp one to take it
off the handles, as it often sticks hard upon them
if they have been greased or wetted. The trouble
of two cloths is very trifling ; spread the dry cloth
open in your le t hand, take hold of the knife
with the damp cloth in your right, then draw
it lightly through the left, and then again holding
it by the blade in the left, wipe it with the right.
Always turn the back of the knives towards the
palm of the hand in wiping them ; this will prevent
you from cutting either yourself or the knife-cloths,
both of which often happen through inattention and
awkwardness. In wiping the forks put the corner
of the cloth between the prongs, to remove any dirt
or dust that may not have been thoroughly brushed
out ; and if there should be silver ferules on the
knives and forks, or silver handles, they must be
rubbed with a piece of leather, and plate-powder,
keeping the blades covered while the handles are
cleaning, that they may not get soiled by the damp
of your hands. If the handles be fluted, let them

be brushed clean. You will find it a great saving of trouble always to wipe your knives and forks as soon as possible after they have been used; as, the longer they are left with grease and stains on them, the harder they will be to clean; particularly if they have been used for acids, or for salads, tarts, &c. Have then a jug of hot water, but not boiling, ready to put them into as soon as done with, and wipe them in the manner before directed. When your knife-board becomes round, or notched at the edges, by using, get it planed, or have a new one, as it is impossible to clean the knives properly if the edges of the board are not square. Let it be kept dry also, and choose your knife-bricks soft and free from knots. It now only remains to direct you how to keep your knives and forks in good condition when they are not in use, as they are things which are very soon spoiled. Rub the steel part with a flannel dipped in oil; wipe the oil off after a few hours, as there is often water in it; and moreover, if it runs upon the hafts, it turns them yellow, and will grow sticky and be hard to get off; or you may dust the blades and prongs with quick lime, finely pounded and kept in a muslin bag. Mutton suet melted is used by some, and bran by others; but bran is apt to attract the moisture from the air; and when you go to your box, thinking to take your knives out all clean and polished, you may have the mortification of finding them covered with rust; and when knives are once rusted it is difficult to keep them afterwards even for a short time without rusting; let them therefore be well oiled and rubbed, and kept in a dry place till wanted. I have been thus particular with respect to the cleaning of knives and forks, because they are things from the appearance of which not only a master and mistress, but every visitor that sits down at table, forms an opinion of the cleanliness and good management of the servant to whose care they are intrusted; and I therefore hope that you will always take care to have them in such a state as may give satisfaction to your master, and be a credit to yourself.

TRIMMING AND CLEANING OF LAMPS.

LAMPS are now so much used in dining and drawing rooms, as well as in halls and on staircases, that it is a very important part of a butler's or footman's work to keep them clean, and enable them to give a good light. I have seen houses almost filled with the smoke from the lamps, and the stench of the oil; and all the glass parts clouded with dust and soot, through the cottons being left too long, or put too high up. This is a most disagreeable thing, enough to make the company cross or melancholy. It is not always a servant's fault that lamps do not burn well; for, unless good oil, and plenty of it, is allowed, no one can make them do so: but it is a servant's fault if they are dirty, or neglected. Where ladies or gentlemen are frequently changing their servants, the lamps are sure to be neglected. Every one who comes thinks they will last his time, and they are thus left month after month with the oil standing in them, till they are quite gummed up, and all the trimming in the world will not make them burn clear when they are in such a state. Whenever, therefore, you go to a fresh place, always examine the lamps; if you find them out of order, and you are not able to put them right, speak to your employers, that they may be sent to a proper place, and made fit for using. If they only want cleaning, pour in boiling water, with a little pearl ash, and shake it well: if the gummy part will not come away with this, scrape it carefully off with a wooden or steel knife; then take the lamp to pieces as much as you can, and clean every part thoroughly. There are generally two or three small holes in the common brass lamps to admit the air; you should be very particular in keeping them open with a pin, or a piece of wire, as otherwise the lamp will smoke, and not give a good light. The patent lamps are more difficult to clean and trim than the common ones. Take them entirely to pieces when you want to clean them, and use nothing but boiling water and pearl ash; as sand, or any thing of that sort, will stick in them so fast, that you will not be able to get it out, and perhaps not to make the parts fit again, as a very little puts them out of order. When you have thoroughly washed the pan which holds the oil, wipe it quite dry with an old cloth, and put it upside down, near the fire, to take off all the damp. Let every other part be done the same. You will find twisting a little tow about in the water and pearl ash in the lamp, with a small stick, very useful in getting off the gummy part of the oil. Do not use sand for the outside of the lamp, any more than the inside; as it takes the lacker off the brass, and makes it look scratched. Flannel and soap are the best things to use. Be particular in cleaning the chimneys of the patent lamps; and also that part which receives the droppings of oil; for if they are not kept clean and free for the air to go through, the lamp will never burn well. Lamps for drawing-rooms and dining-rooms have often from two to six burners; you must be careful, after taking them to pieces, not to mismatch them, as that may cause you a great deal of confusion, when you are in a hurry. The way to avoid this is, to mark the different parts, by tying coloured threads, or any thing of that sort to them. You must take your lamp to pieces all at once, or you cannot clean it properly, as every part ought to be wiped before being put together again, particularly if they are likely to stand some time before they are used. Keep your cottons always clean and dry, as well as the stick that you put them on with. You should choose them of a fair thickness; not *loose*, but *light woven*,

c

firm, and even; get your oil also from tradesmen that you can depend on for letting you have it good, and do not get too much at once, as it loses its goodness by keeping. Cut your cottons even, and fill the lamps with oil when you trim them; but not so as to run over. When fresh cottons are put in, you must let the oil down, so as that they may get well soaked, after which put up the part that keeps the oil up. This must be attended to. Have a tin pot with a long spout to put the oil in with, as without such a one you cannot pour it without spilling, and take care not to spill it over the brass part of the lamps in filling them. Clean the glass part with a damp sponge dipped in whiting, rub it well, but not hard, with a cloth or soft leather, and finish it with a clean linen cloth, or a silk handkerchief, which is much the best. If the brass part of the glass lamp in the hall want cleaning, use soap and flannel, but never sand or scouring paper, and let them all be dusted every day, before you light them. If your patent lamps be lighted up every evening, they should be emptied once a week; do not put the oil that comes from them into the jar with your best oil, but keep it separate to burn in the common lamps. The patent lamp requires fresh cottons oftener, and for them to be somewhat longer than the common ones; in cold weather it is advisable to warm the oil, by putting the lamps near the hall fire, just before you light them; but be careful how you carry them about the house, for fear of spilling the oil. When you

light them, do not raise the cotton up too quick and
high, so as to smoke or crack the glasses. In frosty
weather in particular the glasses are very easily
broken, by a sudden transition from cold to hot.
Raise the cottons therefore gradually, and let the
glass get warm by degrees. Use wax tapers, or
matches without brimstone, for lighting them; but
not paper, as it not only flies about and makes dirt,
but likewise the burnt part of it will stick to the
cotton, and make it burn uneven. If you have any
doubt as to your lamps burning well, light them a
little before they are wanted, or even the night before; for, if any disaster should occur, and you should
not find it out till the company are on the point
of making their appearance, it will cause you great
confusion, and perhaps the breaking of some part of
the lamps in your bustle; besides, as they are often
hung over the dining table, and cannot be reached
without steps, consider how disagreeable it would be
to have to trim them afresh, at a moment above all
others when you have the least time to spare. If
you should be puzzled how to manage any of the
lamps, always ask, rather than run any risk by
guessing about them; and if no one in the house can
tell you, go to some place where lamps are sold, and
there you can get proper instructions on the subject.
It sometimes happens that the links of the chain from
which the different lamps may be suspended, come
open, or the cords wear out, thus causing the lamps
to fall; this you must guard against, by often in-

specting them, and getting them repaired or replaced as occasion may require ; which will be a mere trifle in point of expense; whilst, on the contrary, a handsome lamp falling on the ground, and perhaps hitting somebody on the head in its way, is a matter of no little cost, and may involve a serious degree of danger. — I will now briefly repeat my principal points of advice on this subject. Keep your lamps clean, and the glasses of them bright. Do not let the oil stand long in them, but empty them once a week, and wipe them dry; have good oil, use plenty of it, and keep both it and the cottons clean and in a dry place. You will then, I doubt not, have the pleasure of always seeing your lamps burn beautifully bright and clear, which not only gives a noble appearance to a house, but makes every thing in it look cheerful and agreeable.

CLEANING PLATE.

Is another part of the work of a footman and butler, which requires particular attention. Many are the ways and means of doing it used by different persons, and every one thinks his own the best. Some, however, have much injured the plate intrusted to their care, by making experiments of different kinds upon it ; I shall therefore give you directions both for cleaning it, and for the plate-powder, which it is desirable to clean it with.

In the first place, the plate ought to be free from grease, it must therefore be washed in boiling water, and if it has rough edges, well brushed before you begin to clean it; keep a separate brush for this purpose, and if your other brushes get accidentally greased, wash them well also, or your plate will never look bright. You must exert your own judgment in choosing your brushes for size, according to the pattern and form of your plate; if too small, they will not clean it so easily and well; if too large, they will not go into the crevices, and may run the risk of breaking it, or injuring the workmanship. Your leathers should be soft and thick, the thicker the better; your sponge must be soft, and well soaked in water before you use it, that you may cleanse it carefully from every particle of gravel or sand, as a considerable portion of both is often found in sponges, and if one of this kind be incautiously used, you will find your plate terribly disfigured by scratches, which you will not be able to get out. You may use your plate-powder or whitening sifted through a piece of muslin, either wet or dry; if wet, do not put it on too much plate at once, for, if you let it dry on the plate, you will not be able to make it look well; rub it, if plain, with your bare hand; small articles, such as spoons and forks, you can do between your finger and thumb; if you prefer a leather, keep one for the purpose, but nothing is so good as the hand. The longer the plate is rubbed the better it will look; when you think it is rubbed enough, brush the whitening or powder from out of the crevices and crests of the plate, and from between the prongs of the forks, very carefully. Do not take more than one spoon or fork at a time in your hand, for, if you do, they will rub against each other, and get full of small scratches; neither when you are cleaning them, or at any other time, put them across one another, as the less they are moved or shaken together, the better they will look. Be careful also not to rub the salt and tea spoons, and other small articles, too hard, lest you should break, or at least bend them. Keep a clean leather to finish rubbing your plate with, after it is brushed, and let it be dusted with a linen cloth, before it is put upon the table. Silver dishes, salvers, waiters, bottle-stands, ice-pails, and things of that kind, are difficult to clean, as there is generally a great deal of rough ornamental work in some parts of them, whilst other parts are quite plain; consequently it requires judgment to treat them properly, as the brushes that will do for one part will not do for another. The parts which are rough, or what is called *frosted*, must be cleaned with the hardest brushes; but if the same should be applied to the plain parts around, it would scratch them, therefore you must use your soft brushes for them. The coat of arms, crest, or any other design not being indented so deeply, or raised so much as the edges, do not require so hard a brush, but neither can you,

when you put the whitening or powder on, rub it
with your hand, or the leather; the best wa[?] is to
begin to brush it when wetted, with a soft brush,
and finish it with a hard one; and if this does not
bring the whitening clean out of the crevices, brush
it with a little hot water and soap, then let it be well
dried, and a little powder from a muslin bag shaken
over it and brushed clean off. Dry powder used
with sweet oil makes the things look beautiful; but
they are so much trouble, that I would not advise
you to attempt using it, especially with large things,
unless you have abundance of time at your disposal:
your brushes also must be well washed afterwards,
or they will never be fit for any thing else. The
best way to use it is to put the oil on the plate with
a piece of flannel; then to shake the powder over it,
and rub it with your bare hand till the oil is cleaned
off; the plate will then look extremely well, and
last bright a long time. Plated articles require
even more care than silver ones: they should be
cleaned with soft brushes, not too often, and never
with any thing but plate-powder, not even whitening
by itself; do not wet them more than you can help,
or they will tarnish; nor brush them more than is
necessary, or the silver will come off: the best
thing for them is oil, as I have just directed; and
take care that no plated articles remain dirty or
damp long, for, if they do, they will rust in case
they are plated on steel, and canker if plated on
copper. If they have been used for acids, or if salt be

suffered to remain long upon them, you will find it almost impossible to clean them from the stains, without rubbing off the silver, which is generally very thinly coated on them. You will find a small tooth-brush a very useful size among your brushes, for the narrow parts of your plate, such as toast racks, the legs of casters, and things of that kind, where a larger might only break or damage them. Wash your brushes after your plate is cleaned, with warm water and soap; do them quickly, and then lay them to dry with the wood side uppermost, as that takes the most drying, and the bristles are apt to come out if the wood remains long wet.—I have now, my friends, given you such directions as will, I trust, enable you to lay your plate beside your knives and forks, in a manner equally creditable to you, and therefore I hope you will attend to them, as you may depend on it, you will find your account in so doing.

CANDLESTICKS.

In cleaning silver and plated candlesticks, care must be taken that they are not scratched in getting off the wax or grease, particularly the wax; therefore in cleaning them never use a knife, nor hold them before the fire to melt the wax or grease, as in general the hollow part of the candlesticks towards the bottom is filled with a composition that will melt if made too hot: by pouring boiling water on them you will take all the grease off without injury if wiped directly with an old cloth, and this will save your brushes from being greased, which is too often the case; indeed, you will find it the best way to keep a brush and leather solely for this purpose: let them in other respects be cleaned like the rest of the plate.

Japanned bed-room candlesticks are often spoiled through not knowing how to do them properly, therefore observe, as before, not to hold them too near the fire, or to scrape them with a knife, or put water quite boiling upon them, as this will take off or crack the varnish; the best way is to pour just enough water on them to melt the grease, then wipe them with a cloth, and if they look smeary sprinkle a little whitening or flour, which is the best, upon them, and rub it clean off. It is very seldom that wax candles are put into those japanned sticks to burn, because you cannot get wax off if dropped on them without taking off the varnish. If any of the bed-room candlesticks have a glass, which some have, get the grease off with hot water as before directed, but do not use it boiling, as this might crack the glass; a little wet whitening put on and then rubbed off with a cloth, will remove any smear or dulness. Be very particular in cleaning the patent snuffers, as they go with a spring, and are easily broken; the part which shuts up the snuff of the candles, has in general a small hole in it, where you can put a pin to keep it open while you clean it; be sure to have them well cleaned, that the snuff may not drop about when you use them. The extinguishers likewise must be well cleaned in the inside, and be put ready with the snuffers, that the candlesticks may not be taken up without them. Always have candles set up in the morning ready, particularly the hand candlesticks, as they may be wanted to seal a letter with in the course of the day; the others also ought to be ready, for, if they should be wanted in a hurry, you will most likely break them, in putting in; besides the disagreeableness of keeping your master or mistress waiting, and putting yourself into a great confusion. If the sockets of the candlesticks be too large for the candles, take a piece of paper to put round the end, but do not let it be seen above the nozle of the candlestick. Be particular in putting them in straight, and having your hands clean, that you do not dirty them. Put the finger and thumb of your right hand at the top of the candle, and press it down into the socket, observing to keep the candle upright. Always light the candles to burn off the cotton, before you set them up, but leave the ends long enough to be lighted with ease again when they are wanted. If you have any candlesticks with several branches, you must be very particular in having the candles firm and upright in them, and, if they be too big for the sockets, scrape them carefully, so that you put them far enough in not to endanger their falling out when moving the candlestick: let this rule be observed in all cases. If there should be small china or spar candlesticks kept in the drawing-room for sealing letters, which there generally are, a small wax candle or taper is put into them: if the sockets are too long, as they often are, cut a cork to fit the socket, make a sufficient hole in it to receive the candle or taper, and let a little paper be pasted on the cork, which will make it look neat, and the candle will be kept firmly in. When these candlesticks get dirty, have some hot water to take off the grease. Be very particular in handling those that are made of spar, as they are easily broken, and never put them into boiling water, as it will melt them, nor press the candles tight into the spar, china, or marble, for fear of breaking them. Be very careful to keep your candles clean; for this you should have a drawer or box with a parting, so that the snuffs and scrapings may be in one part, and the pieces of candle in the other. Always scrape the pieces before you put them into the drawer or box, then they will be ready for use. If the candles have guttered down, you should have a smooth-edged knife to take off the wax or tallow, but never use a knife with a notched edge, as it will scratch the candles. If the wax candles should get dirty at any time, or turn yellow, rub them a few times with a piece of flannel dipped in spirits of wine, which will clean them, and make them look well. Always keep the whole candles by themselves, and let the pieces be scraped and put into a drawer or box wrapped up in paper, which will keep them from getting dirty, likewise the snuffs from being broken off too short, which makes them difficult to light, and causes them to gutter as soon as they are lighted.

CLEANING FURNITURE.

Another branch of a man-servant's business is to attend to the cleaning of the tables, sideboard, and mahogany chairs, also trays, or whatever else of mahogany may be used in the parlour or drawing-rooms. You will find, my young friends, that great care is necessary to clean furniture and make it look well. If mahogany has been cleaned with a mixture of a dark colour, and the furniture has got old, it will be impossible to make it look light coloured, unless it is planed; this is not easily done, therefore when it is of a light colour and is to be kept so, you must be very particular in what mixture you put on it, as none which is of a dark colour should be put on mahogany which is intended to be kept of a light colour. If you have two sorts of mahogany, that is, light and dark, you should have two sorts of paste or oil to do them with; but if the dark mahogany is as dark as it is wanted, the paste or oil which is used for the light will do for the dark, as the polish does not consist in its colour; it may, therefore, in such case be used for both, without keeping two sorts.

Keep your paste or oil in a proper can, that you may not run any risk of upsetting it when you are using it. Whether you use oil or paste, you must have two pieces of woollen cloth, one to rub it on with, the other to rub it dry with, to put a polish on; you must likewise have an old linen cloth to finish with, which you should keep for this use only, and not dirty it with any thing else: have a piece of smooth soft cork to rub out the stains with, and use a brush, if the paste be hard, as you will not be able to put it on with a woollen cloth if it is very stiff. Always dust the table well before the oil or paste is put on; and if it should be stained with any thing, rub it with a damp sponge, and then with a dry cloth. If the stain does not disappear, rub it well with the cork or a brush; but let it be rubbed the way the wood grows, for if you rub it cross-grained you will scratch it. Be careful to keep the cork and brush free from *dust* and *dirt*. When you have cleaned the dust off and got the stains out, put on your oil or paste, but not too much at a time; rub it well into the wood; if it is oil, be as quick as you possibly can in rubbing it over the table, and then polish it with another woollen cloth. If you use wax to the furniture, put a little bit on the woollen cloth with your finger, or a small stick; rub it well with this till you find the table looks of a high polish, then have another cloth to finish it with. If you use paste and oil to different furniture, you must have different cloths to rub it with; do not use one for the other, as it will not answer to do so. Be very careful to have the edges of the tables well cleaned, and the oil and wax well rubbed off; if this be not attended to, the ladies and gentlemen will get their clothes dirtied when sitting near the table.

It perhaps will be necessary to wash the tables sometimes; as, where too much wax or oil has been put on, and not well rubbed off, the dust will settle, and you will find it impossible to get it off without. In such cases they must be washed all over with hot beer put on with a sponge or flannel; then rub them dry as quick as possible with a linen cloth, and put the oil or paste on as before directed, rubbing it well in, as they will require more rubbing after washing, but they will look of a lighter colour, and a higher polish than they did before: never let the beer be put on boiling hot, or be left on too long.

Sideboards and cellarets frequently have brass rods, or ornaments of brass, about them, which must be cleaned also; this ought to be done before the mahogany is cleaned, and in doing it great care must be taken that you do not dirty the mahogany. If there is any fly dirt on the brass, take it off with a piece of flannel well soaped, then polish it with the leather you clean your plate with, but do not rub it on the mahogany. If the brass which is on the cellaret has got the lacker worn off, you must polish it with a bit of leather and brick-dust, the same as you do the steel forks; be very careful not to rub the brick-dust into the wood; wrap the leather up in a small compass when you clean it, this will keep the brick-dust from flying about the furniture. When you have done the brass, you must be careful that you do not dirty it with the oil or paste you may use in cleaning the mahogany.

The furniture which is not in constant use will not require to be oiled as often as that which is; once a week will be quite enough; oftener will do it harm rather than good; it ought, however, to be dusted every day and well rubbed; if it be kept covered with green cloth, it will not want so much rubbing. Tables which are used every day must be well rubbed every morning, and great care should be taken to remove all spots out of them, particularly *ink:* this you can do very easily if it is not left to dry in a great while, by putting a little salt of lemons on the spots of ink, then have the end of a cloth just dipped into hot water and rub the salt of lemons on with your finger; this will remove them directly. If you use oil for tables, never let it stand on long, nor put much on at a time, as you will find, if you do, that the damp will rise when hot dishes are put on, or any thing else which is hot. There is less water in wax than in oil, therefore wax is preferable to oil on this account, as you will find it very disagreeable to have much damp to wipe off the table when the company is seated round it, which you will find must be done, or else it will look dull and clouded after the hot dishes are taken off; and it is a sad appearance when one part is of a high polish, and the other looks dull and smeary.

When you clean the tables or chairs, be careful to remove them into the middle of the room, at a distance from the wall, or any other thing which they may stand near, as in many places where I have been I have seen the walls where the tables and sideboard have stood, smeared with the mixture the furniture has been cleaned with; this has not only a slovenly appearance, but likewise disfigures the wall. If the sideboard or side-table is fixed to the wall, you must be the more careful in cleaning it, and roll up your woollen cloth, or whatever you rub it with, tight in your hand, and into a small compass.

LOOKING-GLASSES, MIRRORS, &C.

LOOKING-GLASSES and mirrors generally come under the care of a man-servant; and as they are among the most costly articles of furniture in a gentleman's house, it is of the utmost importance that you should learn to clean them without risk of breaking the plates, or injuring the gilt frames. If they should be hung so high that you cannot conveniently reach them, have a pair of steps to stand upon; but mind that the steps themselves stand steady, or get some person to hold them; for, if you have not firm footing whilst you clean the glass, you will, almost without perceiving it, lean on it for support; and if it be not fixed quite even and firm in the frame, it will break with your leaning upon it. When you find yourself in a safe and proper position for beginning to clean the glass, take a piece of soft sponge well washed and cleaned from every thing gritty, just dip it into water, and squeeze it out again, and then dip it into some spirits of wine or any other spirits; rub it over the glass; then dust it over with some powder blue, or whitening sifted through muslin; rub it lightly and quickly off again with a cloth: then take a clean cloth, and rub it well again, and finish by rubbing it with a silk handkerchief.

If the glass should be very large, clean one half or side at a time, as otherwise the powder blue or whitening will dry on, before you can get it all rubbed, and you will then find it extremely difficult to get off. If the frames are not varnished, the greatest attention is necessary to keep them quite dry, so as not to touch them with the sponge, or with any thing damp, as this will discolour or take off the gilding. To clean the frames, take a little cotton wool, that is, *raw* cotton in the state of wool, and rub the frames with it, as this will take off all the dust and dirt without injury to them; but never use a cloth, as that will hurt the gilding. If the frames are well varnished, you may rub them with spirits of wine, which will take all spots out of them, and give them as fine a polish as though they were just varnished. Varnished doors may be done in the same manner, as it will take off all the dulness from the varnish. Frames which are not varnished ought not to be wetted with any thing, only rubbed with soft cotton wool; and pictures which are not varnished should be rubbed lightly with this cotton wool, or brushed with a feather brush. Never, therefore, use any cloth to the *frames*, or *drawings*, or unvarnished oil paintings, when you clean and dust them.

When you cover up the glasses or pictures in summer, which is in general done, you must be very careful not to injure the walls in so doing, which is too often the case; therefore put a small slip of paper between the wall and each cover of the frame, so that you may pin the paper to it, which you have to cover them with, without sticking pins to disfigure the wall or tear the paper. If the drawing-room curtains are to be covered up, as is generally the case, when the family goes out of town, and the things that they are covered with are old sheets, table-linen, or any thing which is heavy, this of course will pull them out of their proper shape; to prevent which, have some strong paper pasted together as nearly to the shape of curtains as possible; let this be put in the under part of the curtains and pinned to them, then let the cloths which are to cover them be fastened to the top or railing of the curtains and pinned to this paper in the inside, that is, the under part of it; this will keep them in their proper shape and free from dust, &c. But always let them be well brushed and folded properly, before they are covered up.

Packing up glass or china in hampers or boxes requires attention; for, if not done carefully, they most likely will get broken, therefore always have some soft straw or hay to pack them in; and if they have to go a long way and are heavy, the hay or straw should be a little damp, which will keep them from slipping about; of course, the largest and heaviest things will always be put undermost in the box or hamper. Let there be plenty of straw, and pack up the things tight; but never attempt to pack up glass or china which is of much consequence, till you have had an opportunity of seeing it done by some person used to the job, particularly if it is to go a long distance. As the expense will be but trifling to have a person to do it who understands it, and the loss may be great if things of such value are packed up in an improper manner ; therefore never deceive any lady or gentleman in saying you can do it, if you cannot do it as it ought to be done.

***

BRUSHING THE CLOTHES.

In cleaning both your master's clothes and your own, care and attention are necessary to do them well, and so as not to injure them. You must have a wooden horse, which is made for that purpose, to put the coats on, and a small cane or stick free from knots to beat the dust out of them ; also a board or table long enough for them to be put the whole length upon when you brush them. You must have two brushes, one an hard bristle one, the other soft ; the hardest you must use for the great coats, and only for the others when they are spotted with dirt. Fine cloth coats should never be brushed with too hard a brush, as this will take off the nap, and make them look bare in a very little time ; neither can you brush fine cloth so clean with a hard brush as you can with a soft one, as in hard brushes the bristles are thinner than what they are in soft; the hard one will leave the small lint and dust on, when the thicker and softer will take it off and not injure the nap of the cloth. I have found such a brush as is used to shine boots and shoes with the best, as in those the bristles are thicker and of a proper hardness to brush fine cloth coats with, particularly the superfine *blue* and *black* coats. The brush, if it has been used and worn down a little, will be better to brush with.—Be careful in the choice of your stick or cane; do not have it too large, and be particular that you do not hit too hard, to knock holes in the coat, which is easily done if the cane be too large, or if you strike against the buttons; you must always be careful not to hit them, for it will scratch if not break them, therefore a small hand-whip is the best to beat with.

If a coat be wet and spotted with dirt, let it be got quite dry before you attempt to brush it; then rub out the spots of dirt between your hands, but do not rumple it in so doing; if it want beating, do it as before directed; then put the coat at its full length on a board, let the collar be toward the left hand, the brush in the right; brush the back of the collar first, between the two shoulders next, and then the sleeve; let the furthest lapel and arm be brushed first, and then the skirt, observing to brush the cloth the same way that the nap goes, which is towards the skirts of the coat. When one side is done, then do the other; when both are properly done fold them together, then brush the inside, and last of all the collar. When finished, let it be put into its proper place at its full length, if the wardrobe will admit it so. There is no occasion to bear hard on the brush, as by using it quickly and softly the lint and dust will come off with great ease. As some wardrobes will not admit of the coats at full length, and as they must often be packed up into a small compass for travelling, you must learn to fold them so that they may not be creased and rumpled, as that makes the handsomest coat look shabby on a gentleman's back. To avoid this, let the coat be placed as before directed; let the collar be straight, then brush the back part of it first, then between the shoulders and under parts of the arms and cuff, then the top; when done, let it be turned up toward the collar, so that the crease be just at the elbow; let the lapel be brushed next, and turned smoothly back on the arm and sleeve; then brush the skirt and turn it over the lapel, so that the end of the skirt will reach to the collar, and the crease or folding will be just where the skirts part at the bottom of the waist. When you have done this side, do the other the same way; when both are done, turn the collar toward the right hand, and brush the inside which is now the outside. When done, fold one skirt over the other, observing to let the fold be in the middle of the collar; let the collar be brushed the last, and always be kept straight when brushing, and particularly so when you fold the coat. If you attend to the way which I have pointed out, you will find the coats may be packed up into a narrow compass for travelling, without rumpling or creasing.

The waistcoats and small clothes are easily done; but observe, the less they are folded the better, and the more smoothly they are done. If there are separate drawers in the wardrobe for each of the things, let them be kept separate and put in their proper places as soon as they are brushed. In general, gentlemen have drawers or presses for their gaiters, coats, waistcoats, pantaloons, and small clothes, with pegs to hang the boots and shoes on. Take notice, when once showed how they are kept, that you always have them in the same place when cleaned, that the gentleman may know where to find them when wanted, as it may so happen that you may be out of the way when he may wish to change his dress. There should be a brown Holland cloth to cover the coats, to keep the dust from them.

Coats often get greased, and will show the marks if not got out soon. Take off the grease with your nail, or, if you cannot do it so, have a hot iron with some thick brown paper; lay the paper on the part where the grease is, then put the iron or the end of it just upon the spot; if the grease comes through the paper, then put on another piece till you find it does not soil the paper; but if you think that it is not all out, wrap a little bit of cloth or flannel round your finger, dip it into some spirits of wine, and rub the grease spot: this will take it entirely out, if you do it while it is hot. Be very particular not to have the iron scorching hot, so as to change the colour of the cloth, which it will do if you are not careful. You may easily know if the iron is too hot by putting it on a piece of paper; if it turn the piece of paper brown, or scorch it in the least, it is too hot. Never apply fuller's earth to any dark-coloured cloth, as it will take the colour out; but for cloth of a drab colour, fuller's earth is the best, as the hot iron is apt to turn the light-coloured cloth yellow. There are various shades of light-coloured cloth; you must prepare the fuller's earth accordingly: if it be too light, you may put some rotten-stone to make it a darker colour, but if not light enough put some pipe clay to it; let the fuller's earth be well dried before you use it, as it will not easily dissolve without; and when you want it, pour boiling water on it, and let it be put on the cloth while hot, and rubbed into the place where the grease is, then put it before the fire to dry: if there should be candle-grease or wax on the coats, always apply the hot iron with the paper, before you put the fuller's earth on. If at any time the colour of the cloth should be changed, if it is not scorched the air will take it out when it is exposed a little while. White coats may be easily cleaned, if you pay attention to the following directions: To clean them *dry*, you must have some pounded pipe-clay and whitening mixed together ; let this be put into a piece of flannel, or a piece of white cloth, which is much the best ; have some bran to put on the coat, then rub it well with the cloth which has the pipe-clay in it ; this will clean it very soon : the coat must be put on a table, or board to do it with the whitening. If the coat be trimmed with red, you must be careful not to dirty it with the mixture you clean the white with. If the white is to be cleaned *wet*, which it will require in town if worn much, as the smoke makes it very dirty, take some pipe-clay and whitening pounded together, and a little stone blue ; let this be mixed together with some small beer or vinegar, dip a brush into the mixture, and brush it well into the cloth the same way that the nap goes ; it will then look smooth when dry : you may put a little fuller's earth in with the pipe-clay and whitening, which will make it clean better. But if the coat collar and cuffs be red, you must be very particular not to touch the red with this wet mixture, as it will take out all the colour ; or if any grease should get on the red cloth, you must not use fuller's earth, or any thing of that kind, to take it out with, as this remedy will be worse than the disease, for it will be sure to take out all the colour ; the grease must be taken out with the hot iron as before directed, but there will always be a mark left on scarlet cloth if it is only wetted with clean water ; therefore let it be done this way rather than to wet it at all. When the coat is quite dry, you must rub it well to get out the whitening, and likewise you will find it necessary to beat it, to get out the dust. White coats at all times want beating oftener than any other; once a week is enough for others, unless it is summer-time, when it is dusty, or the gentleman wears powder, as too much beating only knocks holes in them and wears them out, particularly if hit too hard, and it knocks off the buttons also. The wet mixture, if properly done, will make the white coats look the best, but always have a ball of pipe-clay by you to rub on when it gets a little dirty, then with a rather hard brush you may make it look tidy directly; but the chief point is in the care you take in wearing it, as some will keep it clean much longer than others. If at any time you should get paint on the coats, you should always have spirits of wine, or spirits of turpentine ready; this with a little bit of flannel or cloth will take it off without much trouble, if not left to get quite dry before you rub it. If you should ever get your hands painted, take a little butter, or any kind of grease, to rub it with; this will soon take it off with washing. Let the plated buttons be cleaned with a damp sponge dipped into plate-powder and rubbed on; for doing these, you should have a thin board with a slit in it made for this purpose; which will prevent you from dirtying the coat in cleaning the buttons, and you will be able to do them better also. Always brush both your master's clothes and your own as soon as you possibly can, and never let them lie about in the dust. Those that are not in use every day should likewise always be brushed and put ready, in case you should want them in a hurry, which is often the case in gentlemen's service.

HATS.

THE hats also want great care, or they will soon look shabby. In the first place, have a soft camel hair brush to brush them with, this will keep the fur smooth without scratching it off; have a stick to put into each hat to keep it in its proper shape, particularly if the hat has got wet; put the stick in as soon as the hat is taken off, and put it into a hatbox, particularly if not in constant use, as the air and dust soon turn hats brown. If at any time your hat should get very wet, you must handle it as lightly as possible, or else you will spoil it; wipe it as dry as you can with a cloth, or silk handkerchief, then brush it with the soft brush, observing to do it the same way as the fur lay before it was wetted, but never use a hard bristle brush to do it with while wet; for, if you do, you will surely spoil it. When the hat gets nearly dry you may use the brush which you have to shine the shoes with, or if the fur sticks so close when almost dry that you cannot get it loose with the soft brushes, then use the hard ones; but if the fur still sticks, you must damp it a little with a sponge dipped in *beer*, or *vinegar*; then brush it with the hard brush till dry. Some persons are so foolish as to advise you not to attempt to touch a hat when wetted till quite dry. If this is right, hat-makers must be wrong; as they first damp them, and then brush them till they are dry, which keeps them smooth; but be careful not to crack or break the felt of the hat when wet, which is easily done if you do not handle them lightly, and be sure to put the stick in afterwards to keep it in its proper shape.

GLOVES.

THE gloves that gentlemen wear are in general of doe or buck skin, such as will wash and clean: if they are white or yellow, they often want washing, and if attention is not paid in doing it, they are soon spoiled. Wash the gloves in soap and water till you have got out the dirt; then stretch them on wooden hands if you have them, if not, pull them out in their proper shape; never *wring* them, as that puts them out of form, and makes them shrink also; but put them one upon another and *press* the water out of them; then rub a proper mixture, for which you will find receipts in the Appendix, over the outside of the gloves; be very particular to rub it between the fingers, indeed over every part of it, or else they will not look well; you must let them dry *gradually*, not too near the fire, or in too hot a sun: this will make them shrink so that you will not be able to put them on; when they are about half dry you should rub them well, and stretch them out, to keep them from shrinking and make them soft; if you let them get quite dry before you rub them, they will be hard and stiff, and be likely to tear in putting on; when you have well rubbed and dried them, take a small cane and beat them, then brush them; when this is done have an iron rather warm, and iron them with a piece of paper over them to keep them from getting soiled; if you iron them with care, you will make them look like new ones; but if you put the iron on them too hot, it will spoil them, as leather very soon scorches and shrinks up.

THE GENTLEMAN'S DRESSING-ROOM.

In waiting on a gentleman, the setting out of his dressing-room forms no small part of a man-servant's business; especially where the gentleman dresses often, and is particular in his things and the way in which he likes them to be put.

In the first place, see that the room is well

dusted and all the slops emptied, and a fire lighted when the weather is cold. Then lay the tooth-brushes, hair-brushes, &c. ready; let the wash-hand stand be open, with a jug of clean water in it; also set the razor-strop, with a bit of paper, or a small linen cloth, to wipe the razor on; let the combs, towels, and whatever the gentleman uses in dress-ing, be ready against he gets up; have hot water ready for shaving; if there be a fire in the room, you can put it by the side, if not, you must keep it down stairs till called for; be careful to have it in readiness. And be very particular to have all the clothes brushed ready and laid in their proper places; if the gentleman gets up soon in the morn-ing, you perhaps may find it necessary to have some of his things brushed and ready over-night, or at least those which he wears in the morning should be done and put ready. Take great care to have the *shirts, waistcoats, drawers, stockings,* or what-ever is washed, well aired before you lay them out for the gentleman to put on, as it too often happens things are sent home from the washer-women very damp. You should have about a yard and a half of brown holland to wrap the coat, waistcoat, and small clothes in; this will keep them clean and free from dust; spread open the cloth, put the clothes in the middle, and turn up the two sides over it; by doing so it will be ready for the gentleman, without his having the trouble of taking it out of the drawers, or its getting dusty: if the gentleman wears powder, a wrapper of this kind is doubly necessary. Before you leave the dressing-room take a view round, to see if all the things are put in readiness, calling them over in your mind,—such as shirt, stockings, drawers, cravat, pocket-handkerchief, coat, waistcoat, small clothes, gaiters, shoes or boots, hat, gloves, &c.; and when once shown the way in which the things are to be put, always do them in future in the same manner, unless ordered to the contrary.

When the gentleman has done dressing and left his room, take the first opportunity of setting it right; let the night-things be carefully folded up and put by for night; put every thing which has been used in its proper place again; let the razor be wiped dry with a soft rag before you put it away, or else it will rust, and wipe it with care lest you should notch the edge of it; wash the hair-brushes and combs when dirty with a little warm water and soap; take a cloth and *wipe* them as dry as you possibly can, then put them a little distance from the fire to dry with the bristles downwards; when thoroughly dry put them into their proper places; never let them get very dirty : let the tooth-brushes and every thing used at the toilette table be put by in their places, clean and ready against they are wanted again; let the towels be hung to dry, and clean ones laid ready; the wash-hand basin be wiped out dry, the jug filled up with clean water, and something put over the top to keep the dust from it. If at any time the gentleman comes home wet, be as quick as you possibly can in getting the dry things ready, that he may be able to change his dress immediately. Let the clean things be well aired, and the wet ones taken to dry; if into the kitchen to dry, be careful that they are not greased, or get dirty in so doing; do not put them too near the fire to scorch; if the coat is new, and a little wet, take a sponge, or brush, and brush it the way the nap goes, then it will be smooth when dried, and will not look spotted; a silk hand-kerchief is a good thing to wipe the cloth with when spotted with drops of wet. If the boots or shoes are very wet, do not put them too near the fire, but let them dry gradually; they should be quite dry before you put the blacking on; let the hat be done as before directed, the fur softly brush-ed smooth, with a stick to keep it in its proper shape, and put it to dry where the dust will not settle on it.

As some gentlemen change their dress twice or thrice a day, if you know the time and what they mean to put on, have the things ready accordingly; but always adjust the room, and put the things in their proper places every time after they are used. Let the water-jug be washed out and dried once or twice a week, otherwise the water will get impure, from the dregs sticking to the sides and bottom, and not be fit to wash in; if there is a glass water decanter, look under the article *decanters* to see how to clean it.

If you have to send the gentleman's linen to the wash, you must be very particular in setting it down; have a small book for that purpose, and likewise note whether the things you send be new or old, as it too often happens that they get changed, or sent home short of the number; therefore always look the things over as soon as they come home, particularly if travelling, or else you will lose your things; when travelling, in particular, look them over before you pay for them, to see if there is any thing missing, and do it while the person is waiting, as you will have no time to be running about after them, when you are perhaps just going to leave the place, nor can you send back for them from a distance, therefore see that they come home right, and in good time, ready for packing. If you have the putting the gentleman's linen out for him to wear, let it be so managed as to have it worn *regularly*, unless he orders to the contrary. If the linen feels damp when it comes home, let it be well aired before you put it away. I shall only add on this point, that whenever you find any of the things displaced, put them in order, and if they should want mending, have them done immediately, or mention it to the gentleman.

PANTRY, &c. &c.

THE pantry is the place where the butler and foot-man in general do the greatest part of their work, such as brushing their clothes, and cleaning plate, &c. &c. Here the glasses, tea-things, and various other things, are kept for the use of the family, and to be convenient to the servant; I shall therefore give you directions how to keep it clean, and properly to time your work *in it*, so that you may not dirty one thing while cleaning another; for it is a disgrace to a servant to have his pantry dirty and in confusion, so that he cannot put a thing out of his hand with-out running a risk of its being knocked down through the confusion of things lying about. Never do any more dirty work in the pantry than you can help; the knives, steel forks, boots, shoes, beating the coats, or any other thing which is very dirty, should not be done in it; as it is most evident that the place where such things are done cannot be a proper one for the tea-things, glasses, table-linen, or whatever may be used in the eating and drinking way, unless the dirty work is done first, and the pantry swept and dusted clean before the other things are set about.

If you have no other place than the pantry to brush your clothes in, they ought to be done the first thing, and put into the drawers or press to keep them from the dust; then clean your knives, forks, plate, and candlesticks, or any thing which makes much dust or dirt, let these be done before you begin to get the breakfast-things ready; but if the family breakfast before you can do this, put your things ready and cover them over with a cloth, then do your dirty work as quick as possible. That you may have the pantry clean against they come down again, take a broom and sweep it, then dust it, and scour the boards or dresser with a scouring brush, or a piece of flannel and soap: this will not take you many minutes in doing, and will give you more room to do your work in, as, when the pantry is clean, you can put any thing out of your hand in a hurry without fear of dirtying it; besides, it is a filthy thing to see the pantry all of a litter and covered with dust and dirt.

You should have a wooden bowl or tub to wash the tea-things in, particularly the breakfast-things, for, as there are plates, egg-cups, &c. with them, the slop-basin is not large enough to wash them in properly; besides, it often gets broken by so doing. This tub, or bowl, should be kept for this purpose alone. It will be necessary to have another to wash the glasses in, as that which is used for the tea-things is apt to get greasy, from the butter, cream, &c. sticking to its sides; and if the glasses be washed in the same, it most likely will make them look greasy also. Never take either of them to wash your hands in. Have a sponge to sponge the water off the board in the pantry, or any other place, so as not to use the cloths to do it with, as they are often spoiled, through being rolled up and put into the drawer without drying; by doing so they soon get mildewed. There should be a small loop to each cloth to hang it up by, if not when used, always spread it open on something to dry. You should have a sufficiency of cloths for the glasses, tea-things, knives, and other things, as there are, or ought to be, cloths separate or exclusively for each thing you have to use them with: for instance, you would not use the cloth which you have to wipe and clean the lamps with, to wipe the knives with, nor the cloth which you use for rubbing and cleaning the furniture, to wipe the tea-things with; nor should you use the cloth which you wipe the tea-things with, to wipe the glasses with, as it will make them look greasy for reasons already explained; therefore use each cloth for its own proper purpose, and not for any other: let them be kept separate, this will prevent mistake; and if you have not a sufficient number for use, always speak to the master or mistress for more, as they cannot know unless they are told; and never make your glass or tea cloths very dirty, particularly the glass cloths. Keep your clean cloths in a drawer by themselves, and the dirty ones in another, observing to let them be dry first.

In washing tea-things, have your water boiling hot, or nearly so; let there be a sufficiency in the bowl, so that you can put them under water; have your cloth in your left hand, then with the right immerge the cup or saucer into it, and wipe it directly with the cloth; by having the cloth open in the left hand and wiping it dry with the right, you will find it will not want hard wiping if the water be quite hot: do not turn them up to dry, as the cook does with her plates; let them be wiped immediately, and the breakfast plates the same. Let the silver tea spoons and forks, if used, be washed also. The tea-pot you must be very particular in wiping, so that none of the tea-leaves shall be left in the pot: if it is silver, let the inside be wiped dry, and handle it lightly, as the handle of the tea-pot is easily broken off: if the spout of the tea-pot gets furred up, have a small piece of wire or wood to push up and down it, but be careful not to break the grate of it in so doing; this will want cleaning often: if the tea-pot is not in constant use, let it be wiped dry and the lid left open, or filled full of clean paper, or otherwise it will soon get musty. If there is a cut glass basin for the butter, or a glass cream-jug, you must wash them with hot water, but not boiling, as this will crack them. You must be very particular in wiping the glass jugs, as the handles easily come off, as likewise do the handles of some of the tea-cups.

TEA-TRAYS.

In cleaning tea-trays you must not pour boiling water on them, particularly on paper or japanned ones, as it will make the varnish crack and peel off, and so spoil the look of them; therefore have a sponge wetted with hot water, and a little soap if the tray be very dirty, then rub it with a cloth; if it look smeary, dust a little flour on, then rub it with a dry cloth. If the paper tray gets marked, so that you cannot get it off as before directed, take a piece of woollen cloth with a little sweet oil, and rub it over the marks; if any thing will take it out, this will. Let the urn be emptied and the top wiped dry, and particularly the outside, for, if any wet is left to dry on, it will leave a mark on it.

WASHING GLASSES.

Put a sufficient quantity of clean cold water into a wooden bowl, or tub, to cover your glasses with, take care not to strike them against the side of the bowl, as they are easily broken: never use any thing of earthenware to wash glasses in, on this account, for if you do but just touch the side of an earthen pan, or basin, it is almost sure to break the glass. If the glasses have been used with any kind of mixture which sticks hard on, you must be particular in rubbing it off before you turn them down to drain; if you cannot get it off with cold water, have some hot to wash them in, but dip them into cold water afterwards, or they will dry too soon, and will look smeary; nor should you let them drain longer than ten or fifteen minutes before you wipe them, for if they do, it will be impossible to make them look well, as they will show where the spots of water have dried on: have two cloths to wipe them with; let the one which is the dirtiest be used just to wipe off the drops of wet with, the other to finish them with. Keep the cloths which you wipe the glasses with entirely for them, and in wiping them let one end of the cloth be in the left hand, let it be open, not twisted; put the foot of the glass into the left hand, and take the other part of the cloth in the right, you will then be able to do them properly, without fear of breaking; but let them be very lightly handled, particularly the small and thin ones; have the softest cloths to wipe those with, and never let them get too *wet*, as they are apt in that case to twist and stick round the glass, which will cause you to break them, therefore dry your cloths, or have fresh ones when wanted. Never let the glasses be standing about when dirty, but let them be washed and put in their proper places immediately.

DECANTERS.

In cleaning decanters the greatest care is necessary, both as to what you clean them with, and likewise that you do not break them, as they are very expensive, yet easily broken. Various are the ways of different persons in cleaning them; some recommend *sand, cinders, coals,* others *egg-shells, wood ashes, scouring paper,* and I know not what. I

have tried most of those things, but I could not
find them answer my expectations so well as I
could wish. In sand, dirt, coals, cinders, egg-
shells, &c. &c. there is a rough scratching nature
which must make them improper for use: you will
find it much better to have some thick brown
paper cut into very small bits, so as to go with
ease into the decanters, then cut a few pieces of
soap very small, and put some water *milk-warm*
into the decanters upon the soap and paper, but
be very particular not to put it in too hot, as this
will crack them: you may, also, put a little pearl-
ash in; by well working this about in the decanters, it will take off the crust of the wine, if
it has not been standing a great while, and give
the glass a fine polish; where the decanters have
been scratched, and the wine left to stand in them
a great while, you perhaps will find it difficult to
get off; to effect this, have a small cane with a bit
of sponge tied tight at one end; this you can
easily do with some strong thread, if you make a
few notches near the end of the cane, that the thread
may hold fast and not slip off; by putting this into
the decanter you will be able to remove any crust
of the wine; but take care not to have the cane and
sponge too large, so as to hurt the neck of the decanter: have corks to put into them while cleaning,
as the stoppers are apt to stick very hard; this will
endanger the breaking of the decanters and likewise
the stopper: let the cane be long enough to reach

to the bottom of the decanter: a strong wire, or small iron rod which you can easily bend, is very useful, with a bit of sponge or rag tied to the end of it to rub the crust from the bottom of the decanter with; this is sure not to scratch them, and I have got off the fur which was on the bed-room water-bottle with it, although it had been on a long time. When the decanters have been properly washed let them be thoroughly dried, particularly if they are not going to be used again for some time, for if they are put away damp, with spots of water in them, it will be sure to mildew them, which will spoil the look of them for ever after: let them be turned down to dry in a proper rack for that purpose; if there is not one, turn them down in a jug, but do not put them on their necks without any support, for any little thing may, in that case, knock them down and break them.

The stoppers are liable to stick in the neck of the decanters, which often causes the breaking of both; to prevent this, when the decanters are clean and empty, wrap a piece of paper round each stopper before you put it into the neck of the decanter; this will keep the dust out, and prevent it from sticking; they will then likewise be always ready when wanted, as it too often occurs, that when they are left out of the decanters they get lost or mismatched. If the decanters have wine in them when put by, you should have some good corks always at hand to put in instead of the stoppers, this will keep the wine much better and prevent the stoppers sticking in, which they will very soon do if wine is suffered to stand in them. This is so common a thing, that I have scarce ever been to a house but what there have been broken-necked or cracked decanters owing to it, always therefore keep proper corks in the cellaret or the place where the wine is kept, as the trouble and expense of a few corks is but trifling, when that of a decanter is great; besides, it keeps the spirit of the wine in better, as it too often happens the stoppers do not fit tight, in which case it soon gets flat. You must, also, consider that when the decanter gets cracked or chipped in the neck the beauty of it is gone, therefore be very particular how you do them.

JUGS AND BASINS.

In most families there are *rich cut glass jugs* and *basins;* the jugs are generally for spring water for the dessert : be very careful in wiping them on account of the handles, mind likewise to have them clean when used, and well *dried* before they are put by ; if they have been suffered to get very dusty, you will find it difficult to clean them ; rub the cut part with a damp sponge dipped in whitening, then take a clean brush and brush it off, but be careful not to strike the edge of the brush against the glass, and wash out the jugs afterwards, as the dust of the whitening will be sure to fly into them while cleaning the outside. The decanters should be washed out before you put fresh wine into them, and, if possible, dried first. Never let them stand about out of their places; as soon as empty, wash them and put them away.

Let all the china jugs or earthenware ones which you have in the pantry be kept clean ready for use, as they may be wanted for beer, water, toast and water, or any thing of this kind; let them be turned upside down to keep the dust out; never let them stand with beer, or any thing else in, long after you have used them for what you want, but wash them inside and out, and wipe them quite dry before you put them away.

CRUET-STAND.

The Cruet-Stand must be looked to every day to see that there is a sufficiency of mustard, oil, vinegar, or any other kind of sauces which there are glasses for; let them be examined and replenished when required, as it too often occurs at dinner when things are wanted from the cruet-stand, that the article asked for is not there, or if it be, that it is not fit for use: it is very negligent in the servant not to look to it before, as there is no time to lose in procuring it while waiting at table, and it is very awkward to see a whole company either going without what they want, or kept waiting by your own neglect, inattention, or forgetfulness of the cruet-stand. If the frame be silver or plated, let it cleaned as before directed under the head *Plate* and *Plated Articles*. The glasses should be wiped and dusted every day, and the mustard-spoon, or any other which is used with the cruet-stand, should be always in their proper glasses and clean. Let the mustard, vinegar, or any thing else which will spoil through keeping, be used in the kitchen before it is kept too long, and fresh put into the cruet-stand: this will prevent any waste, and keep your cruet-stand in proper order. A paper cover for the cruet-stand may be easily made, which will keep it from the dust or being tarnished by the damp air.

TEA AND COFFEE URNS, &c.

If the tea and coffee urns be silver, clean them as before directed under the head of *Plate;* but if they are brown, you will find directions for them under the head of *Japanned Articles;* observe, however, in either case, to let the urn when used be quite emptied and turned up to dry; take the heater out, and put it along with the hook that you take it out of the fire with. You should always have a green baize cover, or a brown holland cloth one, to keep the flies from dirtying it, as their stains are not easily got off; it will also keep it from dust and damp. Be very particular in drying it well if it is not going to be used again for some time, or else it will get musty. You must always

have the urn nearly full of water or coffee if the
heater is very hot, or else it will burn the urn and
do it harm: put the heater in it gently, or you will
in time knock out the bottom of the urn: when
the end of the hook you put it in with is worn off,
have it fresh done, for many urns get spoiled
through using the tongs instead of a proper hook,
by which the heater is let to fall into the urn
with such force as often spoils it.

The mahogany trays which you have to take
up the dinner things in should be cleaned like the
other mahogany furniture, but they will often
want washing if the gravy is spilled over on them;
keep them always clean and hung up in their
proper places.

Let all the drawers in your pantry be kept for
separate uses; keep the clean cloths in one, the
dirty ones in another; in short, have a place for
every thing and every thing in its place, that you
may know exactly where to put your hand upon it,
even in the dark.

You should have a towel hung up behind the
door to wipe yourself with when you wash, for it is a
dirty trick to use the glass-cloths or any other for
that purpose. If you have a sink and a pipe to
take off the dirty water, let it be scoured and kept
clean and sweet. Never throw the chamber ley
down the sink, as it is a filthy trick, and makes a
place not fit to be in; neither empty the tea-leaves

into the sink, or indeed any thing else which is likely to choke and stop up the pipe. I have often seen such things done, but it is a slovenly action, and attended with great expense to the family to have the pipes cleaned and put in order again; therefore, empty the tea-leaves, or any thing of that sort, into a basin or jug, and throw them immediately into the dust-hole.

PLATE.

As the pantry is the place where you keep the plate and other things for the family, which are given into the charge of the man-servant, and he alone is answerable for them, no other servant has any right to go in or take any thing out without his consent, unless it is for the family; as it too often happens that the parlour things are taken into the kitchen, which is one great cause why so many of them get broken and spoiled. If there is not a sufficiency of kitchen utensils, let the cook ask for more; if she will not, you must for your own sake; for, if there are not necessary things for use in the kitchen, it is natural to suppose that the servants will take the first thing they can get hold of; thus the best knives and forks get spoiled, and the glasses broken. I know in some families they will not allow servants a sufficiency of things to use in the kitchen and likewise to do their work with; but, my young friends, you should always ask for such as are really necessary for use; and then if your em-

ployers will not allow you them, it will not be your
fault if other things get broken or spoiled in consequence; but if you have proper things for use,
recollect that it is your duty not to lose or break
them. Be very careful not to expose your plate in
the pantry or kitchen window, particularly if
fronting the street; many servants, by foolishly
doing so, have lost the plate and their place also. I
often see a quantity of plate exposed for hours in
windows which face the street, probably from the
vanity of the servants to show how much they are
intrusted with; at any rate it is great inattention in
them, as thieves are desperate and wicked enough
without doing any thing to tempt them. If your
pantry is facing the street, put a cloth over the plate
if you think it can be seen by the passers by. Always keep the plate-chest and the drawers which
you keep your plate in locked, and the cupboard
shut which you keep the glasses in, particularly
while doing any dusty work. If you should live
in a place where the kitchen-maid or house-maid
has to clean the floor of the pantry, you had
much better do it yourself, it will not take much
time, and will spare all words and contention
about it, as the maids in general have enough to
do; besides, you will naturally be more careful
not to do any injury, or misplace your things.

BREAKFAST, &c. &c.

I SHALL now, my young friends, give you a few
directions how to set out your breakfast-table,
and likewise the *lunch*, *dinner*, and *tea*. But
I shall first speak of the breakfast. I shall suppose that you have all things clean and ready for
use, and that the party at breakfast consists of
four persons; put the green cloth on the table,
then the linen one on that; if it should be too
large, let one end of the cloth be turned smoothly
under on the green cloth; this is better than
turning up the four corners and setting things on
them, such as the salts or plate; as the cloth may
be suddenly pulled, and then the things will be
thrown down. Have four tea-cups and saucers,
and if there be coffee, four coffee-cups and saucers;
also let there be a cream-jug, a tea-pot, slop-basin,
sugar-tongs, and a tea-spoon for each cup and saucer both for coffee and tea, also spoons for the
egg-cups, when used, with a butter-knife; and if
meat is eaten, proper knives and forks to cut it
with. You must set a plate and a knife and fork
where each person is to sit, then put the cups and
saucers as conveniently as you can for the person
who makes tea; let the cream-jug, slop-basin, and
tea-pot, be put just behind them, the cream-jug to
be to the right hand, the slop-basin to the left, the
tea-pot between the two; let the bread, butter, and

meat, or any thing else, be arranged as conveniently
as you can. Always have salt on the breakfast-table;
and if the family like mustard, &c. to their meat,
the cruet-stand likewise. Sometimes the meat and
other solid things are put on the side-table or tray
close to the breakfast-table; if so, let a cloth be put
on, and the things placed in it with knives and
forks proper for carving, with the cruet-stand, &c.
Have the tea-caddy near the person who makes the
tea. Let the chairs be put round the table, and in
cold weather have the fire made up and every thing
in its proper place; and when once you are shown
the way the family like, keep to it in future.
Always have the water boiling and the iron quite
hot for the urn; put the water into the urn before you put the iron in, and let it be nearly full,
or the heat of the iron will spoil it. Be careful
that you do not put any water into the place where
the iron goes, as the steam may fly into your eyes
when you put the iron in, and blind you. When you
take up the urn, do not forget the urn-rug, if there
be one used; let the urn be put just behind the
tea-pot on the table, so near that the person who
makes tea can turn it into the pot without getting
up to do it. If you have buttered toast to make,
let the bread be toasted as quick as possible, in
order that it may be light; but if you have to
make dry toast, and that very thin and crisp, toast
it some time before it is wanted, and put it into the

toast-rack before the fire; but if the toast is pre-
ferred thick and not very dry, do it quickly and
not till it is wanted. When you take any thing up,
always put it on a waiter, never take it in your
hand. When you take away, first take the urn,
then have a tray to put your other things in; be
careful not to break them, by putting too many on
it at a time. When you have removed all the tea-
things, &c. take the linen cloth off the table, but
do not roll it up like a pocket-handkerchief and
then put it under your arm, as this will be sure
to rumple it: let your arms be expanded as wide
as you can, take hold of the ends of the cloth and
turn it over smoothly; you may then put it under
your arm without fear of rumpling it. If the green
cloth is removed also, take this off in the same
way; let them both be folded up directly that you
get down stairs, and in the same creases they had
before. Let the linen cloth be put into the press,
and the green cloth into a drawer, to keep them
from the dust. Next put away the bread, butter,
meat, and any other eatables which may be left,
in their proper place; then wash up the breakfast-
things in boiling water, or nearly so, and in the tub
or bowl which you have for that purpose. Let the
tea-spoons be washed the first, the tea-cups and
saucers the next, then the plates, and afterwards the
silver forks; do not put glass cream-jugs into boiling
water, or boiling water into them, as it will break

them; it should be hot, but not boiling. When you empty the tea-pot, wash out all the tea-leaves, and wipe the tea-pot quite dry if silver, as I have before directed, and when done, let all the things be put in their proper places.

As in most small families the table linen is put on the table more than once before sent to the wash, if you have different cloths for breakfast, lunch, and dinner, and perhaps one for supper, or tray-cloths, let the breakfast-cloth be put into the press over-night, ready for morning; when this is taken out let the lunch one be put in; and the dinner one next, and so on; thus, you will always have your cloths neat and in readiness. Sprinkle a little clean water over the cloth with your hand, but do not make it too damp, or sprinkle it in too large drops at a time, as it will take off the gloss, and may likewise draw the stains out of the wood and stain the cloth. If at any time you should forget to put the cloth into the press in proper time, or have but little time to let it stay there, damp it with warm water, putting it into the press, and pressing it tight down, which will make it smooth in a very short time.

LUNCH.

WHERE there are children, they often have their dinner at the time their parents take their luncheon, in which case the cloth is in general put on the table,

and some have it always laid for lunch. If there is
any kind of meat brought up, have the salt, some
dessert spoons, and a few large ones, with the carving knives and forks, if any thing to carve, and small
knives and forks to eat with ; have spring water, or
toast and water with rummer-glasses, wine-glasses
one for each person ; set ready the chairs, and make
the table look neat. If both hot and cold provisions
are used, have hot and cold plates : if pies and
puddings, let a dessert-spoon be put for each person;
the small cheese-plates in general are used for lunch,
as they take up less room. If the family have their
lunch on a proper lunch-tray, which opens and shuts
up with small hinges or springs, you must be very
careful not to overload it at any time, for fear it
should fly open and the things fall out and break.
Have a cloth over the tray, and put your things on
it, as you would on the table : when full, turn up the
ends of the cloth smoothly over the provisions, then
fasten up the sides of the tray and carry it up; put it
on the table which is intended for it, then put down
the sides of the tray and properly adjust the things,
so that they may be convenient. If there is no green
cloth on the table, never push the tray along it, for
if there should be the head of a *nail* or *screw* in the
under part of the tray, it will make an incision in the
table and spoil the look of it. Most trays of this sort
have a green cloth pasted under them; if at any
time you should find it gets loose, have some strong
paste and fasten it on again. Some families have

nothing for lunch, but bread or biscuits, and a glass
of wine; in this case a small tray will do, with a
napkin on it.   It is very seldom that the servant is
required to wait in the room at lunch, unless the
younger branches of the family dine at that hour;
but be sure to have a sufficiency of things for use:
you may soon learn what is necessary if you pay attention. When all are done with, take the things
down and put them in their proper places; fold the
cloth carefully up, and if there is any plate dirtied,
wash it up and put it into its proper place: if you
have not time to do it just then, put it in a cloth and
lock it up; never leave it lying about, as in the daytime there are persons coming backwards and forwards to the house on business, or there may be
workmen about, whom you may not know much of;
besides, we should not expose the honesty of any
one to temptation.   Let your glasses be washed up,
your knives wiped, and every thing put away that
has been used, in order that you may have a clear
place to set your dinner-things ready, and have the
glasses, &c. clean.

Some staircases are so narrow that it requires
great care to take the tray up without defacing the
walls by knocking the paint off, or scratching them.
Be careful to *fix* your *foot firm* upon the steps, to
secure the safety both of your own limbs and of the
things which you carry; never set any thing on the
stairs, for fear any person should fall over it, as
fatal accidents have arisen from inattention in this
respect.   E 3

DECANTING WINE.

BEFORE we begin with the conducting of the dinner
I shall make a few remarks on decanting wine,
as this is a thing in which many gentlemen are very
particular.

In the decanting wine you must be careful not to
shake or disturb the crust of it, when you draw the
cork, or move it about, especially Port wine. You
must have a good corkscrew, and a wine-strainer,
with some fine cambrick in it ; never decant wine
without this, to prevent the crust and bits of cork
going into the decanter. Let your decanters be clean,
and, when you draw a cork, put the bottle on the
floor, place your feet at each side, then take the
corkscrew in the right hand, and with the left press
the bottle firmly on the floor, keeping it upright,
which is easily done by putting the left hand on the
neck of the bottle: the corkscrew should be put
quite through the centre of the cork, or else you will
break the cork in. If you have to move Port wine,
you will find it best to keep the same side uppermost
which was in the cellar; this in general is marked with
a stripe of white. When you decant Port wine, you
ought not to drain it too near ; there are generally
two thirds of a wine-glass of thick dregs in each
bottle, which ought not to be put in, but in *white*
wine there is not much settling ; you must be careful,
however, not to let what little there is go into the

decanter, as it is much finer than the dregs of the
Port : when you decant it therefore, you must pour
it off slowly, and raise the bottle up gradually ; the
wine should never be decanted in a hurry, therefore
always do it before the family sits down to dinner.
If there be company to dinner, and several sorts of
wine should be wanted, you must be very careful
not to mix them, or label them incorrectly; for, if you
do, it will cause sad confusion ; you will not be able
to know the different sorts of wine by their colour;
therefore, to prevent mistakes, have a number of
written labels if you have not enough of silver ones,
to put on all the bottles, and let those which are un-
drawn be labelled as well as those which are drawn ;
this will be the surest way to prevent mistakes : the
written ones you can make a slit in, to let the
neck of the bottle through. If there should not be
decanters enough, to hold a sufficiency of wine for
the company while at dinner, and for the dessert also,
take out the corks as before directed and put them
lightly in again, and let your wine-strainer be in
readiness, that you may have nothing to do but to
pour it off when wanted ; this will keep you from
being in a flurry and making it thick while doing it.
Be careful not to jostle the decanters against each
other when you move them about, as they easily
break when full, and likewise not to place them in
any situation that may endanger their safety; put
them in a place where you can lock them up. If the
weather is hot, you must keep the wine in a cool

place till wanted ; if it is very cold, and the company like the chill taken off, let it stand a little distance from the dining-room fire, but most likely your employers will tell you when they wish this to be done.

DINNER-TABLE.

IF one part of a servant's business calls for greater attention than another, it is waiting at table; it is a branch likewise, wherein he can show more of his *ability* than in any thing else he may have to do, as many make great pretensions to cleverness in conducting a dinner, who yet never knew the first principles of properly waiting at table. This causes great unpleasantness in a house, both to the family and the rest of the servants. It is no easy thing to be able to wait at dinner well, and have every thing done in proper and systematical order. I am sorry to say, that there are but few servants who can manage a dinner party of twelve or fourteen, without confusion in some part of it or other, particularly in small families, where they have not company very often ; confusion likewise often occurs through the room being too small, or not having a sufficiency of things for the party without having to wash up some while at dinner, or, as it too often happens, through the person who is at the head of the family, not knowing his business well. The greatest attention is necessary, in properly arranging the things for use, and *appointing* each one his *place*, and what he is to do while waiting; for, the greater the number to wait, the greater will be the confusion, if their offices are not properly arranged before the company goes into the room. One clever servant that understands his business, will get through more than two awkward ones, who are ignorant of it; but still the best servant may have more assigned to him than he can accomplish, to the satisfaction either of his employer or himself. A family generally thinks that a footman may wait well enough on six persons; but this is too many to be comfortable with, if there are many things to change.

Always inquire of the cook what there is for dinner, as by doing this you will be prepared to know what things you want, and have them in the room ready: it is very awkward to leave the room in the middle of dinner, for things which ought to have been in before it was set on the table; besides which, they often get broken, by catching them up in a hurry. When you have learned what there is for dinner, ask if there is any particular way of sending things up, without which you may make sad confusion, likewise have a bill of *fare*, that you may not be at a loss to know how to put the things on the table, for some families will have the sauce and vegetables put on the table with the meat, &c. while others will not; the manner of putting on the dishes, likewise depends greatly on the will and pleasure of those who order the dinner, but then it is quite necessary that you should know the particular ways of the family (if they have any), and adopt them accordingly.

CLOTH.

In putting on the cloth, let the table be dusted, and the green one put on first, then take the linen one, observing to have it the right side outermost; this you may easily tell by the hemming and the fold of it: be likewise particular in having the bottom of the cloth face the bottom of the table, as in most families they have some design woven in their table-linen, such as their crests, or coat of arms. If the pattern be baskets of flowers, the bottom of the basket must be towards the person who sits at the bottom, as the design should always look up the table. The middle of the cloth ought likewise to go exactly down the middle of the table. If there be *mats* to put under the dishes, let them be put even in their proper places. If there are napkins for dinner, you may fold them up various ways, but let them be done neatly, so that you can put the bread in for the person conveniently; if the crest, or any other particular design, is worked in the napkins, fold them so that it shall be seen. When you have laid your napkins round the table, then lay the knives and forks at proper distances from each other; let the knife be put to the right hand, and the fork to the left of the person, but do not let the handles of either reach beyond the edge of the table; let the carving knives and forks be set at top and bottom of the table, on the outside of the other, and the same way in length: when this is done, put the plate on the table. If the salt-cellars be silver, let a table-spoon be put on each side of them, as they are in general oblong: let the nearest to the carving-knife be put with the handle towards it, and the other the contrary way; let the gravy-spoons be put beside the carving-knife, and laid the same way: if fish and soup, the fish-knife at top, and soup-ladle at the bottom; let the handle of the fish-knife be put near the end of the carving-knife, *cross-ways*, and the soup-ladle the same, as they will be more handy this way. Put a table-spoon for each person, beside the knife, with the handle within one inch of the edge of the table. Next put on the water bottles and glasses. Let a wine-glass be put to the right hand of each person. If there be glass coolers for the wine-glasses, let them be filled about two thirds with spring water, and the wine-glass turned up in it; let those be put about three inches and a half, or four inches, from the edge of the table to the right hand of the person, with the foot of the wine-glass toward the edge of the table. If the wine decanters be put on the table, if there be four decanters of wine and two water-bottles, let the wine be placed near the four corners of the table, but not too near. This you will be able

to judge, as it depends a great deal on the size of
the table, but you must so arrange them, that they
will not be in the way of the dishes, in taking off and
putting on, nor yet too near the edge of the table, for
fear of having them knocked off. Let the two water-
bottles be put in the centre of the flanks of the
table, that is, between the two who sit at the side of
the table. Let a small rummer-glass or two be put
with each of the water-bottles; those you must so
arrange as not to be in the way of the flank dishes,
or to be inconvenient to the company who sit at the
side. If the family dine by candlelight, the candles
are in general put in the centre of the table, or if
there should be two branches, the salad, or *epergne*,
will be put in the middle, and one of the branches
between this and the top and bottom dish; but it is
very seldom that an *epergne* is put on a table for so
small a party as six, particularly where there is but
one servant to wait; therefore consider what number of different joints and dishes there may be, and
likewise whether it is likely that any other person
will drop in just at dinner-time, as in some families
this is often the case, and proportion your plates, &c.
accordingly. If there be many changes, you should
have six large plates for each person, with pudding
and cheese plates, and as many knives and forks;
but a little experience will teach you the best as to
these things, for some persons will use half as many
more as others will; but observe to have a few
more than you want, rather than not enough. Have

2

three wine-glasses for each, and at least two rummers; always have one or two more in case they
should be wanted, or any accident should occur;
do not, however, take a great many more things
than are wanted, for fear of breaking them or
scratching the plate, which is easily done in moving
it about, if great care is not taken.

THE SIDE-BOARD.

In setting out your side-board and side-table, you
must study convenience, neatness, and grandeur,
as you cannot think that ladies and gentlemen have
splendid and costly things without wishing them to
be seen or set out to the best advantage. I have
seen some side boards and tables set out in such a
way as to look all in confusion, when, if they had
been properly arranged, they would have looked
beautiful. Some persons will put on their things
with such taste and neatness, that it will strike the
eye of every person who enters the room with a
pleasing sensation of elegance. The glasses which
are to go on with the wine and dessert, and all the
glasses which are used at dinner, must be kept on
the side-board. In some families there are blue
hock glasses and small liqueur glasses used for dinner; when these are not wanted on the table, you
may ornament your side-board with a few of them,
as they will have a pretty effect among the rest: if
there is bottled ale, cider, &c. you must have the

proper glasses for it. Two rummer-glasses each
will be enough if there is no bottled ale, cider, porter, &c. If you have not plenty of glasses for
use, ask your employers for more; if they will
not let you have a sufficiency, this is not your
fault, but never attempt to make three or four persons drink out of one glass, as that is a filthy trick.
Now, with the glasses and the small waiters, cruet-
stand, sugar-basin, and the cut glass water-jug,
which is to go on with the dessert, and a few silver
spoons, you will be able to set out your side-board
to advantage; but never put any silver forks, or
steel knives and forks on, as they will scratch it;
let these be put upon the side-table. If you have a
lamp or candle for the side-board, put it in the
centre close to the back, then it will not be in your
way in taking the things off. If you have different
sorts of glasses for use, let the best and handsomest
be for the dessert, and put them at the back part
of the side-board, and those for the use of dinner
in front, so that you may have them at hand. In
setting out your side-board, you ought always
to contrive your things so that you can have them
as you want them without reaching over any thing
else; it is two to one but you may break or
knock some down, if you have to reach them in a
hurry. Let the beer-glasses, rummers, and all
glasses of this kind, be put on one side, and the
wine and small liqueur glasses on the other. As to
the form or design in putting on the things, this will

in some measure depend on the shape of the side-board ; but with the generality of those which I have seen, it looks the best to have the glasses to form a half circle or crescent. As the lamp or candle will be in the centre of the side-board at the back, begin there, and place them to within three or four inches of the front ; but if the side-board is very large, you will have no cause to take the whole sweep of it, for if it does not look full enough, you can put the finger-glasses along the ends of it. If there is any difference in the size of the wine-glasses, let one of each sort be put to each person for the dessert. In forming the half circle or crescent, let the highest glasses be arranged the furthest off, and the smaller ones in an inner circle ; let them be put two and two, that is, one large and one small, that you may have them quite handy to put on the table when wanted. In the space between the glasses put the cut glass water-jug, the cruet-stand, sugar-glass for dessert, the decanter-stands with the wine which is for the dessert, with the small hand-waiters ; let the water-jug, sugar-basin, and cruet-stand, be put down the centre, and the de-canters and stands on each side of them ; let the waiters be put near the edge, in front of the board, as they will be often wanted ; if there is any space left, ornament it with a few spoons, as silver sets off glass, and makes the side-board look well. Let the wine-glasses be to the left hand, and the beer-glasses, &c. to the right of the side-board, when you

face it; you will find this the most convenient plan,
as you hold the glass in your left hand when you pour
out the beer, &c.; but always contrive to set your
beer, spring-water, toast and water, or any thing
of this kind, in a tray or cellaret, or else have a
knife-cloth to put underneath the side-board to put
them on, that you may not dirty the room; put
them as near the glasses as you possibly can, and
likewise your plate-basket for the dirty plates, with
boxes and trays to put the dirty knives, forks, and
spoons in; let those be put in the most convenient
place : have a separate tray for each, or one which
has partitions in it, as the spoons ought to be put
by themselves, and the others the same; this will
prevent the plate being scratched, for, if the knives,
forks, and spoons, be all put into the same tray,
they will be sure to be so.   You must have a small
tray with a clean knife-cloth in it, to remove the
carving knives and forks from the dishes before you
take them off the table.

THE SIDE-TABLE.

On this the cold plates, cheese-plates, and dessert-
plates, are put; also the salad, vegetables, and
meat; the steel knives and forks and the silver
forks. Let these be so arranged as to be handy, and
also to look ornamental, as well as the rest of the
things, observing the same rule here as on the side-
board, to have that which is wanted first the nearest

towards you. Let the d'Oyleys be put into the dessert-plates, with a proper dessert-knife, fork, and spoon to each. If the finger-glasses go on when the cloth is removed, let one be put on each plate; then let the two knives be on the right side, and the spoon and fork on the left of the person whom you set it before. If both steel and silver dessert-knives are used, place one of each on the plate. Let the water be put in the finger-glasses ready. If the side-table is too small to hold all the things, and you have room on the side-board, let the dessert-plates be put on each end of it. Have the steel knives and silver forks so placed and arranged, that you can be able to take them without noise and confusion when you change the plates. You will always find a sufficient quantity of things to set out your side-board and side-table with, therefore study convenience and elegance in putting them on, and do not be afraid of a little trouble when there is company to wait on, as, when the side-board and side-tables are set out with ingenuity and taste, it has a very pleasing effect in going into a room where order and design prevail. Whether you have few or many at any time to dinner, make it a matter of thought how you can manage and arrange your things to the comfort of those you serve and your own convenience, not forgetting the appearance, as I am sure, my young friends, that you may unite the three together.

It is too often the case, where there are plenty

of things both for use and ornament, that the side
board and table have been in the greatest confusion
through the idleness and carelessness of the servant.
The place where the side-table should be put depends on the form and size of the room : if it be
long and narrow, the side-board in general is at one
end and the side-table at the other ; in all cases,
the best situation is near the door. Always contrive
your dining-table that you may be able to go round
it when waiting, without running backward and forward, as this often causes confusion and accidents ;
and put the plate-basket and knife-trays near each
other, but not so as to stumble over them while you
are waiting. Do not bring the cheese into the room
till wanted, as the smell of it may be disagreeable
to some of the company.

DINNER.

Having got most of your things ready, I shall
now consider the dinner ordered, as it in general
takes the cook half an hour to dish it up, which gives
you time to get the rest of your things into the
room, and others done which would not be proper
to have been done before; such as the bread cut and
put round with the plate and dish warmers, lighting
the lamps and candles, and having proper lights
in the passages, that you may see how to go on, and
not knock the tray against the wall in carrying it
up, which often causes the gravy to be spilt, or the

things to be broken. In many houses there are little steps and narrow passages to go along to carry the dinner, which are very badly lighted up, thus causing many accidents. It is highly necessary to have a good light in conveying the things backwards and forwards to the dining-room; but some families, who are on the save-all plan, will grudge sixpenny-worth of oil, or a candle, and lose a poundsworth in breaking of china, &c.: if you, however, are allowed to light up properly and do it not, it is your own fault if any accident occurs through the want of light. Get your beer, soda-water, ginger-beer, porter, spring-water, &c. ready. If the weather is warm, you must put the ginger-beer in a cool place in the room, and it ought to be kept in a cool cellar just before it is wanted, as the warm room will make it fly about, and perhaps on the company. As soon as you have put all your things ready, take your tray to the kitchen to put your dishes on; let your tray-stands be in a proper place, and if you can be any assistance to the cook in helping her to dish up, and you have all your own things ready, do it. Let your plates be quite hot, and always dust them before you put them to warm. If there should be no fire in the dining-room, you must warm them in the kitchen; but be very careful in carrying them up stairs, that you do not let them fall out of the plate-warmer. See that the door of the plate-warmer is fastened, and keep it towards you, with one hand under the bottom, and the other on the top. Never risk the handle alone, as I have known many accidents occur through it; do not put too many plates one on another, as they will often break this way: neither overload your tray with the dishes, but rather go twice than run a risk of upsetting them. Let the soup, or any other dish which is likely to slop over, be carried up by hand. In carrying up and putting on, you must be as quick as possible, not to let the dinner get cold before the company sit down.

If you have four corner dishes with top and bottom, let the top and bottom dishes be put at regular distances from the ends of the table, leaving quite sufficient room for the plates; if the table is not too small, let them be in the centre, and the corner dishes on a line up the side, and at equal distances from the edge of the table. Let the dishes on each side answer each other as to distance from the edges and top and bottom dishes. If you should have flank dishes, those in general project a little wider, as they come just in the centre of 'the table on each side the *epergne*, candles, or salad-bowl. By casting your eye up and down the table, you will soon discover whether the dishes are set in a proper line and at equal distances from each other; if they are not, those who sit at the top and bottom will perceive it in an instant.

As the first course is put on the table before the company come into the room, you will be able to arrange it properly, which will be a guide to you in the after courses; as there will be the impression on the cloth where the dishes have been removed from. It is very seldom that there are more than the top and bottom and two side dishes for six persons to dine off; but whether they are few or many, they must be set at proper distances from each other and from the edges of the table.

Notice the different ways in which different persons carve particular joints. Let the heads of fish be put to the left hand of the carver, and the heads of hares, rabbits, and roasting pigs: in an aitch-bone of beef let the silver skewer which is in general put into it be towards the left hand; a quarter of lamb, let the thin part be put from the carver toward the centre of the table, with the neck end toward the left hand; with shoulder and leg of mutton let the shanks be put towards the left hand, and a haunch of venison the same; hams are in general served up in the same way; but there are three or four ways of carving them; put them however with the shank part towards the left hand, unless otherwise ordered. Turkies, geese, ducks, fowls, pheasants, woodcocks, snipes, partridges, and all sorts of game, are put with the heads towards the right hand, as they are best to carve this way. Some, however, will have the turkey, goose, and duck with the head toward the left hand, on account of getting at the stuffing. In the sirloin of beef let the thick bony end be to the left hand; the saddle or chine of mutton, let the rump end be toward the left hand. In many dishes there is a place for the gravy to run into; let this end of the dish be always toward the right hand of the carver; as he serves the gravy with the right hand. If at any time you do not know which way a dish should be put on, ask the cook rather than make a mistake and have to turn the dish round after the company is set down, for this looks very awkward.

When the dinner is on the table let the plates be put round, one for each person; let the soup-plates be all put at the bottom of the table, a little to the left hand of the person who helps it, and close to the tureen; this will be more convenient than putting the soup-plates right in front, both to you and the person who serves. Let the bread be put round before the company comes in, as you will have no time to do it afterwards. Where there is but one to wait, he has enough to do to hand the plates to the company. You cannot carry the bread in one hand and the soup in the other to do it properly, and a number of accidents occur through attempting to do more than one person can do well. When you have put the plates round and the dishes are on the table, see if you have the sauce-boats with the gravy and sauces in them, the vegetables, salad, and cold meat, if any, and if every thing is in its proper place. When all is quite ready, go up as

4

quick as possible to announce dinner; but do not just go to the room door and there bawl out, " Dinner is ready, Sir," or, " Ma'am; " but if the room is large, go a little way towards your master and mistress, and say, " *The dinner is served, Sir;* " speak in an audible manner, but do not bawl aloud. When you see that your master or mistress has noticed the announcement of dinner, go and open the dining-room door ; you must stand behind and hold it till the company have gone in, then shut it; if the door will stand open without, you must stand in the hall just on the outside. As soon as the company are seated, if there is soup, take the cover off; if there be only fish at the top and a joint at the bottom, remove the cover from off the fish and the sauce-boat which belongs to it.

While waiting at dinner never be picking your nose, or scratching your head or any other part of your body, neither blow your nose in the room ; if you have a cold and cannot help doing it, do it on the outside of the door; but do not sound your nose like a trumpet, that all the house may hear when you blow it; still it is better to blow your nose when it requires, than to be picking it and snuffling up the *mucus*, &c. which is a filthy trick. Do not yawn or gape, or even sneeze, if you can avoid it; and as to hawking and spitting, the name of such a thing is enough to forbid it without a command. When you are standing behind a person, to be ready to change the plates, &c.

do not put your hands on the back of the chair, as it is very improper, though I have seen some not only do so, but even beat a kind of tune upon it with their fingers. Instead of this, stand upright with your hands hanging down or before you, but not folded. Let your demeanour be such as becomes the situation which you are in. Be well dressed, and have light shoes that make no noise, your face and hands well washed, your finger nails cut short and kept quite clean underneath; have a nail-brush for that purpose, as it is a disgusting thing to see black dirt under the nails. Let the lapels of your coat be buttoned, as they will only be flying in your way. You should have no buttons underneath the sleeve of the coat, as they are apt to strike against the glasses, or pull things down.

If there be only yourself to wait, take your standing at the bottom of the table with your back toward the side-board, about half a yard behind the person who sits at the bottom, and a little to the left hand. By doing this, you will be able to command a full view of the whole table; whereas, if you stand right behind the person who sits at the bottom of the table, you cannot well see when the plates want changing. When you hold a plate for the carver to put any thing on, let it be in your left hand, holding it even with the rim of the plate on a level with the rim of the dish or tureen, or, if any thing, a little lower, and close to the dish: this will make it convenient for the carver to put on what he is carving without soiling the table-cloth. If the dish have no place for the gravy to run into, take hold of the plate with your right hand and hold the dish a little up with your left, so that the gravy may run to the other end, that the person who carves may serve it with his right hand: never put your right hand under your left to hold up the dish, as, if you do, you may have the gravy spilt over the sleeve of your right hand, or on the cloth. When you take hold of a plate, do not put your thumb half way into it, this is very disagreeable and improper; there is a rim to all plates, let your thumb be placed on it, and the fore finger a little turned toward the thumb with the next to it drawn in, so that the end of it will come to the hollow or thick part of the thumb with the other two fingers drawn to the thick part of the hand, then press your thumb and your two fingers together, and you will be able to keep the plate even and without risk of its falling or turning aside; or if you cannot manage to do this way so well, let your thumb be on the rim of the plate, with your fore finger a little turned in, with the others a little contracted and bearing against the swell of the plate close to the rim, pressing, as before, your thumb and fingers together. When you hand a plate to the person whom it is for, take it in your left hand and put it down be-

F

fore him on the left side, unless at some particular times you will find it necessary to set it down with your right, and on the right side.

When you have held the plate to the carver, perhaps you will have to take it to one who sits at the side, for something that is next to him; in that case take it in your left hand to the left side of the lady or gentleman, and never attempt to go on the right, as this is very improper. In handing the vegetables and the sauce-boats about, always take them to the left side of the person with your left hand; put a large spoon in the vegetable dish when you hand it; if there are two sorts of vegetables in one dish, have two spoons; take the dish in your left hand; let your thumb be only just on the rim, but you will find it necessary to have firm hold of it with your fingers underneath; if it is too heavy for one hand, put the other under the dish, when you hold it for the company to take it out; or if you can just lodge one end of it on the edge of the table, this you can hold with one hand, and it will be more convenient to the person you take it to. You will in general find that you must hand the vegetable dish endways; let the spoon be put accordingly; let the sauce-boats be handed the same, with the proper sauce-spoons in them. You can hand two small vegetable-dishes or two sauce-boats at a time, or bread with either; but when you are handing round the plates, you cannot well do so. Take the covers from off the dishes with the right hand, if on the right side, and the left if on the left side; be quick in turning the cover up, so that the steam or water may not drop and dirty the cloth, which it will if you do not pay attention, particularly if the inside should be a little dusty, which sometimes is the case; this, with the edges of the dishes, you will do well to look to, for sometimes the cook is in such a bustle as to forget it.

When beer, water, &c. are called for, take hold of the glass with the left hand; but do not put the foot of the glass between two of your fingers, and your thumb on the edge at the top where the company are to drink from, as it is not cleanly so to do, but take hold of the foot of it with your fore finger and thumb, and keep it upright by pressing your finger against it underneath. If you are serving porter, and it is liked with a froth on it, by pouring it from the pot in a small fine stream, a little distance from the glass, you can froth it up as much as you like; but do not pour it over the sides of the glass, for, if you do, it will drop on the ladies' and gentlemen's clothes while drinking; if you should slop the outside of the glass, take another; never offer one to any person while the wet is dropping off it. When you have filled the glass about three parts full, put it on a waiter and carry it in your left hand, to the left side of the person who has called for it; put it near the edge of the waiter, and then put your thumb on the foot to keep it steady; but in a

little while, with practice, you will carry it best
without putting your thumb on it. Always, in carrying any thing on a waiter, walk quick, and take
short steps; you will soon be enabled to serve
quickly. As it sometimes happens that the chairs
are set so close together that you will find a difficulty in holding the glass for the person to take it,
observe to have the glass and waiter as before directed, and let your left foot be advanced toward
the chair or table, so near that you can lean forward on your left, rather sideways: by doing so
you will be able to hold it so that the person can
take it with ease and pleasure: do not throw out
your right leg when you are leaning forward, but
keep both your feet pretty near together. When
the person has taken the glass, fall back on your
right foot while he is drinking; when done, lean
forward on the left again to take the glass; this
you can do without moving either of your feet,
if you get sufficiently near to the back of the chair.
Take the glass, when done with, back to the side-
board, and place it so that you will know it again,
that the same person may have it a second time
if wanted; but if another sort of liquor should be
asked for by the same person, you must not use
the same glass, but get a clean one; for instance,
you would not use a glass which has had toast and
water, for wine and water, or presume to make
three or four persons drink out of one glass; never
do so, but always keep the glasses separate. If at

any time you should not have enough beer, or toast and water, in the room, when called for, never do such a filthy thing as to empty it from the bottoms of the glasses which have been left; you should always arrange with your fellow-servants on such occasions as those, to get whatever you want for you, without your having the inconvenience of leaving the room. Never take a glass of beer, or any thing else, to the company, without putting it on a waiter; and when you take any thing from off the table, such as the glasses or spoons or small cruets, have the waiter in your left hand, and take them off with the right; and if the company should at any time want a knife, fork, or spoon, and not a plate, always put them on the waiter or plate, to hand them to the person; but do not put the glass on the waiter when you want to pour the beer or toast and water in, for fear of slopping the waiter; and if you should at any time slop it accidentally, wipe it quite dry; keep a cloth for this purpose, and a clean one in case any glass should want to be wiped or rubbed.

If there be ginger-beer, soda-water, or spruce beer for the company, when you are to serve it, put the glass on the right hand side of the person who wants it, on a small waiter; turn your back towards the table while you draw the cork, and ease it a little at a time, to prevent it from flying about the room, or on the company. If the neck of the bottles is small, have a small corkscrew, for a large one will break the cork in pieces, and mix it with the liquor, which will be very disagreeable; let the cork-screw be put in the centre of the cork, and turned quite through, this will prevent its breaking. Always serve ginger-beer, soda-water, or any thing of this kind, while it is in a state of fermentation, or else it is not good. If there should be more than one person at a time who want it, and one bottle holds enough, let the glasses be all quite ready for each person, that you may let them all have it in a state of effervescence; you therefore must be quick in doing it; but do not put your thumb or finger in the neck of the bottle while you carry it to the others when you have served one, but have a cork in your hand to put in if wanted, which it will be, unless you are very quick, or else it will get flat; but keep the ginger or spruce beer in a cool place, if in summer, till wanted; they never ought to be made too long, for, if they are, it will be almost impossible to prevent them flying about when you draw the cork: it is the best for two persons to serve such things, as one can draw the cork and pour it out, while the other holds the tray with the glasses on, and then hands it to the company, which will be the most convenient to all parties.

Now, Joseph, as we left the company seated at their dinner, when we turned aside to have this conference, we will take another turn to them, as I have no doubt but they will be glad to see us, as we only uncovered the soup and fish. If there is any remove for the fish or soup, ring the bell, that it may be in readiness; the company seldom have any vegetables with their fish, but they sometimes have sliced cucumber; if so, do not forget to hand it round with a silver fork and spoon in the dish; if there should be any left, put it on the side-table, to go on with the cheese. Before you remove the fish and soup from off the table, take the small tray with a clean knife-cloth in it, hold it in your left hand, and take the fish-knife and soup-ladle off with the right; be careful in doing it; hold the tray as near as you can, that you may not dirty the cloth. As soon as the removes are put on the table, uncover all the dishes unless otherwise ordered; if they are not silver covers, you may put one into another and take them all out of the room at once; make as little noise as possible, and be sure not to set them down in the room, to fall over them. When you have handed the meat, be as quick as possible in handing the vegetables and the sauce-boats round, as it too often happens that the sauces are forgotten and the company will not inquire for them for fear they should ask for any thing which is not in the room. Keep your eyes open to see what is wanted, and your ears also. Do not wait to be asked for every thing by the company, as you may see when they want bread, vegetables, and sauce, and likewise what may be wanted on particular occasions; such as mustard to duck and goose, fish-sauce to the fish, mint-sauce to the lamb, bread-sauce to fowls, &c. &c. Keep your eyes on the table also to see when the plates want changing. Be deaf to all the conversations of the company, and attentive only to their *wants*. Never be seen listening to what the company are talking about, and neglecting your own business, which too often is done by servants. When you hand a glass of beer, toast and water, or any thing else of this kind, it is the proper way to wait till the person has drank it, then take the glass away; but you must deviate from this rule sometimes; for instance, if there be plates that want changing, or others to be served with any thing, you can easily remove the glass off the table when you have done serving the others: this the family must put up with, where there is only one to do all. When you change the plates, put them softly into the platebasket, that you may not break them; and the knives and forks into the separate trays allotted for them, making as little noise as possible. When you take a full plate to any person, and there is an empty one before him, let the full plate be in the left hand, and take the plate from before the person with the right *first;* by doing so, you will be able to do it without confusion, as you will find it rather awkward to do, until you have practised it. Always put the clean knife and fork into the clean plate; when you put it before the person, do not take the plate in one hand, and the knife and fork in the other. You may generally know when a person has done with his plate by his putting the knife and fork alongside of each other across it. If there should be two sorts of vegetables in two different dishes, you may take one in each hand, or the bread, or sauce-boat; but not to have the plate in one hand, which you are going to put before a person, and a vegetable-dish in the other; for how can you take the empty one from before the person if both your hands are full?

In putting on the dishes and taking them off, I shall observe to you a few things, as many accidents have occurred through inattention and want of care. The first course is put on in general before company come into the room, but the others of course must be put on afterwards. When you take off the dishes, do it with both your hands, standing on the left side of the carver; let your right hand be about half way up the side of the dish, toward the carver; and the left, one third of the way up the side which faces the centre of the table; let your thumbs be fixed firm on the rim of the dish, and your fingers underneath; lift the dishes high enough to clear the glasses, &c. that you may not knock any thing off, but do not heave them so high as to endanger the joints falling off, and do not snatch them off the table, but take them steadily. The side dishes are not so heavy and large as the top and bottom dishes, therefore you will be able to

take them off with one hand, but have firm hold
that you do not turn them aside, for you will find
more difficulty in taking off the side dishes than the
top and bottom dishes, as you will have to lean over
the chairs of those who sit at the sides ; if you turn
yourself sideways you will be able to take them off
with more ease; never attempt to take the dishes
from off the table standing on the right-hand side of
the carver ; put them on the same way as you take
them off, on the left side of the carver ; take care to
hold the dish firm, and keep it even, that you may
not spill the gravy. When you perceive that the
company do not seem inclined to eat of the dishes
on the table, you must keep your eye on your
master, or mistress, to receive the signal when to
remove the first course ; and you must, previous to
your going to wait at dinner, arrange with the cook
that you will let her know a little before you begin,
that she may be ready with the second: be very
particular not to forget this; if you do, the cook
cannot be ready, and the company will be kept
waiting through your neglect ; and if, at any time,
you see that the first course is likely to be done
with sooner than it in general is, be sure to let the
cook know of it as soon as you can, by ringing the
bell, if you cannot get to speak to her.

THE FIRST COURSE REMOVED.

As soon as you receive the signal for removing
the first course, take the small knife-tray with a

clean knife-cloth in it, and take all the carving knives, forks, and spoons which have been used, from off all the dishes, before you attempt to take the dishes. Observe when you take off the knives, forks, and dishes, to begin at the bottom of the table, and take the knives, &c. from the left-hand side of the dish, and go regularly round, removing from off the sides as you go up and down the table; then, when come to the bottom where you began, put down your tray, and begin removing the dishes from off the table in the same way you did the knives, forks, &c.; remove the bottom dish first, then the side, top, and the other side: as you must consider in taking off and putting on, you should lose no time, nor be running backwards and forwards any more than you can help; let your dishes be taken off and put on in a systematic order, so that you make no bustle and confusion in the room; be *quick*, but *quiet*, in your movements; as you take off the dishes, put them into a large tray, which of course you will have ready, and if there is no one to take them down stairs for you, do it yourself; empty your tray as quick as possible, and put the second course on it; but be not in too great a hurry, as you may spill the gravy, or break the dishes, but be no longer than you can help in carrying the things up and down. It sometimes happens, when there have been but four dishes for the first course, there have been six for the second; be particular in putting them on; have the bill of fare

in the tray, or on the sideboard, then you will be
able to look at it, and prevent making mistakes, as
it is reasonable to think that ladies and gentlemen
like to have the dishes put on the same way which
they have contrived for the things to answer each
other.   If you were to pay attention in setting the
dishes in the tray, you could place them in it as
they are to go on the table; this certainly would be
an advantage to you, and you may easily do so
when you have the dishes all up; begin to put
them on in the same order as you took the
others off, the bottom dish first, then the left side,
and top, &c.; be very particular to have them
in a proper line with each other, and at *equal
distances from* the *sides* and *ends* of the table.
When you have put them all on, take the covers
from off those which are covered, then be ready to
wait on the company; when you see they are
finishing with the second course, let the cheese-
plates be put before them as you change the others,
a small knife, and if there is salad, a fork also
should be put in the plate.   Have your cheese and
butter and salad all ready against the second course
is done with; take it off as before directed; be sure
to remove the knives, forks, &c. &c. first; then, as
soon as all the course is removed, put on the cheese,
&c.; if there should be two cheeses and a salad,
with sliced cucumber and butter, let the cheeses
be put top and bottom, the butter in the middle,
with the salad and cucumber on each side; let the

cheese and butter knives be put with the cheese, the spoon and fork with the salad, and a spoon with the cucumber. While the company are eating their cheese, take all the loose knives, forks, and spoons off the table, and put the glass-coolers with the wine-glasses on a small tray, which you ought to have in the room ready, not to have to move them three or four times, as this takes up time, besides running a risk of breaking them: wine is seldom drank with the cheese, only porter, ale, or something of that kind, therefore take all the wine-glasses and put them into your tray to remove them with the rest. As soon as the company have done with the cheese, remove it from the table; then take all the things quite off, both dirty and clean; have a spoon (if there is not a proper table-brush) with a plate, and take off all the bits of bread, then with a clean glass-cloth and another plate, brush all the crumbs off the cloth; as soon as this is done, put round the finger-glasses, one to each person. If you have not got the dessert ready before you put the finger-glasses on, you had better get it while they are using; during that time, likewise, remove as many of the things as you possibly can out of the room. As soon as the finger-glasses are done with, remove them; then take off the cloth with the green one also, and put them out of the room at once, other-wise it is very likely in your haste you may fall over them; when you have removed the cloths, if the hot dishes have drawn out the damp, take a cloth and wipe it off, but do not do it with a dirty cloth, as this will not be pleasant for the company to see, nor yet use your best glass-cloths to do it with, as the table mats may have been cleaned with oil, or wax, which will come off on the cloth and make your glasses smeary; therefore have a cloth for this purpose, and do not use it for any thing else. As soon as you have wiped the table, put the dessert on; put the dessert dishes nearer the middle of the table than you did with the meat, &c. &c. as they are smaller. Observe the same rule in putting on the dessert as the other courses, unless there are more dishes in the dessert than in the courses; in this case, you may put on the dessert dishes top, middle, and bottom, before you put on the sides; when they are all put on, then put on the sugar-basin and the water-jug, between the top and bottom dishes and middle one, in the same line; then put the cut-glass rummers between the two side dishes and the middle, two on each side; then put the wine-decanters on at the bottom of the table, next to the gentlemen; but if there be none but ladies, put the wine near the one who sits at the top. Let four table-spoons be laid to serve the dessert with, and if there be a cake, let a knife be put with it; next put on the dessert-plates, and two wine-glasses to each person; and when the dessert is all set out, be as quick as you possibly can in removing every thing out of the room except the clean glasses on the sideboard, the cruet-stand, and the clean plate; the clean knives, forks, and plates on the side-table may also be left; but remove all the dirty plates, knives, forks, beer, toast and water, &c. &c. All things of the eating and drinking kind should be removed before you leave the dining-room; but let it be done quickly, and with as little noise as possible, so as not to appear all in a bustle and confusion when leaving the room, for a good servant is *to have every thing in the room ready* when called for, to put on and take off the dishes in order and without confusion, to be quick in changing plates and handing vegetables, or whatever may be called for, and never want telling what he ought to do. The sooner you leave the room after the dessert is put on the better; never loiter about the room when the company are drinking their wine; some servants that I know will be rattling the knives and forks, and removing all the clean glasses,. &c. &c. from the dining-room before they leave it, but this is quite unnecessary. You may leave the sideboard and side-table to look ornamental without much trouble or loss of time.

If the family do not dine by candlelight, perhaps by the time dinner is over it will be necessary to light the lamps in the hall and on the staircase; have all the candles and lamps in the drawing-room in readiness, if not lighted, as the ladies seldom stop long in the dining-room. As soon as you have removed all the things which have been used for dinner, see that there be water boiling for the tea

and coffee; let the iron heaters be put in the fire for
the urns, and all things which will be wanted for
tea in readiness: then put all your things into their
proper places; let the steel knives be wiped, and
the plate washed and wiped quite dry; the glasses
likewise washed and put in their proper places;
this will make room for the dirty glasses you will
have when the dessert things are removed, and the
tea-things done with; always keep the pantry as
clear as you can, that you may have room to put
things out of your hand, without confusion or fear
of breaking them.

If at any time you should not have wine
enough out, and more should be called for, try to
catch your master's eye, if you cannot provide it
without him, and then go out of the room. If,
after waiting a few minutes, you find he does not
come, go back again and tell him, that a person
wishes to speak to him. Never say, " There is no
more wine out," or any thing of that sort, as, if
you do, you will make yourself appear very ignorant of proper behaviour, and render your master
liable to be ridiculed for your want of consideration.

TEA.

If the lady makes tea in the drawing-room,
which with small parties is generally the case, have
the tea-tray well dusted, and the tea-cups and
saucers put on, one for each, with a tea-spoon to
each; if there be coffee, a coffee-cup and saucer for

each, with a spoon to each; let the tea-cups and saucers be put on the near side, so as to face the person who makes the tea, with the tea-pot, cream-jug, and slop-basin on the off side; and let the tea-caddy be put near; if there be an urn-rug, do not forget it. If you have to wait at tea, that is, to hand it about to the company, you must have a small hand-waiter; if there is not one proper for the purpose, use the one with which you hand the glasses about at dinner, as you do not require a large one. When you take away the tea-things, always take the urn off the first, then put the tea-caddy into its proper place, and then remove the tea-things. Always have a cloth in your pocket to wipe the table with, in case it should be slopped, or crumbs of bread, &c. left on, and properly adjust the candles, if there are any on the table. Perhaps you may have to carry the tea and coffee up stairs to the company ready-made; if so, you must be careful not to slop the tea over the cups into the saucers; see also that you do not forget the spoons, sugar-tongs, cream, or slop-basin; have a tea-pot on the tray with hot water in it, in case any of the ladies' tea should be too strong. Your tray ought to be pretty large, so that you can put the bread and butter, sugar-basin, or any thing else upon it; take care to arrange them so, that the ladies may take the cups with ease, and hold the tray low enough for that purpose; if it will not hold enough to go once round, you must serve it as far as it will go, and then get more. If you have not cups and

saucers enough, you must wait in the room till the
company have done with some of them. Be quick
in taking up the tea when it is once poured out,
that it may not get cold before the company have it,
which is a subject of complaint almost to a proverb;
you will easily know when they have done, by their
putting the spoon in the tea-cup, or refusing it when
you offer it to them. If there should be a fire in the
room, look at it before you leave the room.

WAITING.

I will now, William, attend to your account of
the accidents that you complain have befallen you
in waiting, as it is very probable, that by telling
you what occasioned them, I shall be able to prevent your having them happen to you again.

William. Well, Sir, as I was one day waiting at dinner, a gentleman called for some pudding;
he was deeply engaged in talking to the person on
his left hand, and rather leaning, so that I could
not put it down on that side without disturbing
him, I therefore tried to put it before him on the
right; in doing which, I hardly know how it happened, but, while I was setting it down, the gentleman rose up in his chair and stuck his elbow
into the pudding, and sent part of it tumbling on
the floor. My master began scolding, which, together with the thoughts of the accident, quite
upset me, so that I broke some glasses, and did
many more awkward things in my flurry and confusion, for in fact I scarcely knew what I was about.

Onesimus. Now, James, let us hear what you have to say on this subject.

James. Oh, Sir, what happened to me was ten times worse than William's accident, at least it was so to me. A gentleman having called for a glass of porter, I carried it to him; but he being busily employed talking to a lady on his left side, and rather leaning towards her, did not see me; I, being in a hurry, as some of the company were calling for things, went to his right hand side and just touched his arm with the waiter; he turned quickly about, capsized the porter over my light-coloured small clothes and white stockings, and sent the glass rolling about the floor; so you may think what a pretty plight I was in, and what my feelings must have been when I was in this condition before the company, and particularly as I thought I was a little to blame.

Onesimus. I really think you both were to blame. Pray, just answer one question, William; did you hand the plate of pudding with your right or left hand?

William. I attempted it with the left hand.

Onesimus. I thought so. Pray, had you ever any more accidents by setting the plates before the company on that side?

William. Why I cannot say but I have had. I was once changing a plate, and, in putting it down on the right hand of the person, I struck it against the glass-cooler, which you know stands on the right hand side of the person, broke it and set the water running about the table and down on the floor. In removing some of the dishes likewise from off the table, on the right side of the carver, I had nearly capsized a wine-decanter once; but I knew, when I reflected on what you had told me, that it was my own fault, and I then made up my mind not to do so again.

Onesimus. Certainly; you never ought to attempt to put any thing down before a person on the right side with your left hand, nor to put any thing, or offer it, on the left side with your right hand, as this is very awkward, and is often the cause of accidents. But observe, if at any time you find a person in deep conversation with any one who is on his left hand, if you have a plate in your right hand, you may with care put it down before him; but never attempt to do it with your left, as this is back-handed. I do not wish you to make a common practice of doing so, but sometimes you will find it necessary to take every advantage you possibly can in waiting, only be careful and quick, and move with caution. As to your being flurried by the accidents happening and your master scolding you, this is not to be wondered at. I am sorry when any lady or gentleman does so, as it only makes things worse; but you must always endeavour, when you have a misfortune, to keep yourself as quiet and cool as you possibly can. Whether it should be your fault or not, never attempt to defend yourself on such occasions, whatever your employers may say; if it is not your fault, take another opportunity of proving it. Sometimes, when I have been leaning over some of the company to put a small dish on the side of the table, it has dropped in two, and I have found one part of it in my hand, while the other and the contents have been upon the table-cloth or the floor. This was the cook's fault in not seeing that the dishes were perfect before she sent them up; therefore, when you have dishes to put on the table, keep good firm hold, and let your fingers go under the bottom to prevent an accident.

As to you, James, I am much surprised to think that you should ever attempt to push a gentleman's arm with the waiter when you were serving the beer: this is what you never ought to do; for, when a person calls for any thing, and you take it to him and find he is busily engaged in talking, never interrupt him. If it be to the person on the left hand of him, and you are wanted at the same time to serve others, have the waiter in your left hand, and take the glass with your right hand, put it down before him, then attend to the others; or, if he should be talking to one on his right side, you can put the glass before him with your left hand, having the waiter in the right. I hope, therefore, you never will again bob or push any person's arm when you hand any thing, as this is very rude: not that it is quite proper to take the glass off the

4

waiter and put it before any body ; but where there is not a sufficient number of servants to wait, you had better do this than for the rest of the company to be calling for things and no one to serve them ; you must, therefore, watch every opportunity in handing and managing for the comfort of those you serve, as well as for your own benefit, as a great deal depends on good contrivance at those times.

And now, William, tell me how you managed the large party you went to the other day to help to wait.

William. Sir, I can assure you that I never got into such a bustle and confusion in all my life before. Sometimes I was sorely vexed, at others I could not help laughing ; and I think, had you been there, Sir, you would have laughed to see the awkwardness of the persons, and the disasters which befel us.

Onesimus. I think, William, at such times laughing is not at all allowable ; indeed it is always very improper for a servant to be laughing before company. But proceed, William.

William. Well, Sir—there were fourteen at dinner, and six servants to wait on them. There was one of the best of dinners provided for the company, but I think the worst of waiters. There were the butler and boy, with the groom who belonged to the family ; also a hired waiter, and an-·other footman besides myself : this footman and I had never been in the room before we went into it to wait; of course we did not know how the things were placed, or any particular ways of the family. This footman, indeed, knew very little about waiting at table, as he had been only a short time in place. The butler was a man not much experienced in service, and the boy quite young; and the stablemen you know are generally very awkward. I myself felt rather confused in first going into the room, not knowing where to put my hand on the things when wanted, as I should have done had I been shown them before the company had gone into the room.

The dinner being ordered, we were all hands aloft to take it up; and when it was put on the table the butler went to announce the dinner served. When he came down, he perceived some of the candles in the dining-room were not lighted: this caused a little bustle to get it done. The company being seated, and the soup-covers removed, the confusion began, as there was nothing appointed for us to do in particular, or even where we were to stand. When we had served the soup round, I took my station just behind my mistress, at the lower end of the table, and the other footman just behind his. They were both sitting close together, and of course we were standing nearly together. The butler and waiter were at the bottom of the table, the boy and groom at the top. The soup being done with, it was removed for the fish. Here we were all servers of fish, but forgot the sauce till several called for it at once: this set us all running one against another to hand it. The cucumber was forgotten in the bustle; and there were some persons of title at dinner who ought to have been served first, but we, being almost strangers, did not know them. When the company began to call for wine, beer, &c. our confusion increased: some running to fetch things in a hurry ran against each other; by so doing, the knives and forks and plates were tumbling about the room. While one was stooping to pick them up, another was running to fetch something else, and tumbled over them. The footman, hastening to take a plate to a gentleman, and not looking before him, ran his head into the face of the hired waiter. Sometimes there were two or three trying to change one plate; sometimes one would take the dirty one away, while another would be taking the clean one, and putting a knife and fork with it where there were both before; or sometimes a fork; while another, seeing that there was a fork, supposing there was a knife also, would not take any: by doing so, some of the company had three or four knives and forks, while others had not one.

Onesimus. Now, William, I shall ask you a few questions first, and then I will give you and James further directions as to the management of a dinner-party. Was there one knife and one fork for each person when they sat down to dinner, or two knives and forks?

William. Two, Sir.

Onesimus. I thought so: this is one cause of the confusion, as it very often happens that the company only use the silver fork in eating the fish and some other things; when this is the case, there will be two knives left and but one fork: now, unless the same person who takes the dirty plate away likewise brings the clean one, it is very likely to make mistakes, as, not knowing whether the knife is dirtied or not, you may take both a knife and fork; and if there should be only one wanted, it is very disagreeable, for, if you want to hand any thing about, it is inconvenient to have it in your hand, and to run to put it on the side-table causes great loss of time. There never ought to be more than one knife and fork put to each person in so large a party, unless it should be properly arranged before the company comes into the room, that every servant who changes the dirty plate shall also take a clean one, or that one should take away the dirty plate while the other should put a clean one in its place. It is solely the want of method that causes so much confusion, as each ought to have his proper place appointed, so that a servant who is on one side of the table shall not be running to change a plate which is on the other. Let every person, therefore, have his proper station where to stand and whom to wait on, and keep his eyes and ears open to their wants: I do not say he ought not to assist the others if need requires, but he ought to

G

pay particular attention to those he attempts to wait on. And now, William, how did the butler remove the carving knives and forks, and spoons, and likewise the dishes? and how did he put the second course on the table?

William. Why, he took the small knife-tray which has the knife-cloth in it, went to the top dish, and took off the knives, forks, &c.; then came back to the bottom dish, then up to the flank dishes. He observed the same rule in taking off the rest of the dishes, and likewise in putting on the second course; and when he was removing the carving knives and forks, he made the boy follow him up and down, which had a very droll appearance. I told him, after dinner, that I thought he had run backwards and forwards more than he had any occasion for, as you had always told James and myself not to make any parade or bustle, or run about more than we could help, at dinnertime; but he seemed to think his own way the best, and being " only a lodger," I said but little, and laughed heartily after all was over at the scene which I had witnessed.

Onesimus. This shows you, William, how obstinate some persons are in their own conceits. We often see the Wise Man's proverb fulfilled; for there is more hope of a fool than of a self-conceited person, who is so wise in his own eyes. Some servants imagine that their master and mistress will think them good servants because they are always

on the run and bustling about: if there are such
gentlepeople, I am sure, when they get such servants as those, they will pay for it in the many
things which oftentimes are broken through it.

I shall now proceed to give you and James directions how to manage a party of fourteen to dinner, to which I hope Joseph, John, and Edward,
will pay attention. There are many things more
to be done in a party of fourteen than in a party of
six, as it requires great attention to proper management. I shall observe a few things : If you
have any Dukes, Earls, Lords, or any persons
of title, to dine, you should be very particular to
serve them according to their priority of rank;
therefore no one who does not know them personally should be allowed to hand the plates, but only
the sauces, vegetables, bread, &c.

GETTING READY FOR DINNER.

As a party of fourteen requires a long table,
and some rooms are very small, you must, if possible,
contrive to have a free passage round it, or else this
will be very awkward. Be particular in having the
design of the table-cloth to face the person who sits
at the top of the table, as it often happens at
those large parties that the table-cloth is left on for
the dessert : when this is the case you will have
narrow slips of table-linen for the purpose, or napkins, to put down the sides of the table and across
the bottom and top; they are to keep the cloth

clean for the dessert, and when the dinner is over they are removed. You will want eight salt-cellars for fourteen persons, and six water-bottles. If the table is large enough, and not over-crowded, in a party like this you will have a *platcau* or *epergne* for the centre. If you have two sets of finger-glasses, and lip-glasses for the company to wash their mouths in, put the lip-glasses and one set of finger-glasses in a tray, if you have not room on the side-board or side-tables, then you can bring them into the room when wanted. In general, with so large a party as fourteen, there will be two soups and two dishes of fish: be sure in that case to have two soup-ladles and fish-knives, and a double set of carving knives and forks. Be very particular in looking to your cruet-stands, to see that every thing is good which is in them, and that they are well cleaned. Let your table be laid early in the day, and every thing done which can be got ready, as on company-days you will find more answering the bells and the street-door than at other times.

I shall consider that you have got all things ready in the dining-room and for dinner; which you could get in the fore part of the day; and I shall now consider it to be six o'clock, and the dinner ordered at seven. At six o'clock see that the plates are warming, the iron heaters for the dishes put in the fire, the water on to put into the hot plates; get the spring-water for the water-bottles, and like-wise for the cut glass jugs; have the beer, soda-water, &c. in readiness, and let the bread, salad, and cucumber, with the cold meats, be put on the side-tables ready.

Half past Six o'Clock.

Begin, if dark, to light up your lamps and candles; be sure to have plenty of lights in the passages, pantry, and other places which you may have to go through; get the dish and plate warmers ready on the table, the bread put round in the napkins, and the chairs set round the table in their proper places. When the cook has dished up the dinner, be quick in putting it on the table, that it may not get cold. If you have ice-pails to ice the wine, let this be done; be careful not to dirty the pails in putting the ice in. Let a hot plate be put round to each person, and the soup-plates to the left of the persons who serve at top and bottom, pretty near the tureen. Take a view round the room, to see if every thing is in its proper place. As it depends upon you, William, to conduct the dinner, you will have time to look over the table and on the side-board and side-tables, while the rest will bring up the things to you. Do not flurry yourself in running up and down stairs to fetch things; the others must do that, as they have no particular charge upon them, and you will have the care and arrangement of the whole: therefore keep yourself cool and collected, as your head on such occasions must work more than your hands.

Having now brought you, William, to the setting on the first course, and every thing in readiness in the dining-room, we will proceed to the arrangement and waiting at table.

The first thing which you should do is to appoint a person to assist you in handing the wine, and taking the things from off the table and putting them on. I shall suppose that James is fixed on for this. You, William, should stand a little to the left of the carver at the bottom of the table, and have one waiter to the right of the carver, then he will be ready to take any thing from you, and hand it to the persons whom it is for. You, James, take your standing to the left of the carver at the top of the table, and have a waiter the same as William : let the other two stand opposite the middle of the table, one on each side. You, William and James, should hold the plates to the carvers, then give them to the other persons who wait, for them to hand to the company. Let each one have his own side to wait on, so as not to be running round the table : let those two persons who assist you at top and bottom, be the persons who shall fetch up the dishes, &c. and hand them to you ; they ought to look over the bill of fare, and be perfectly acquainted how it is to go on the table, or they cannot hand it properly. If those two persons have the bill of fare, they can set the dishes on their trays as they are to go on the table ; the covers will be on the dishes, which will prevent you from seeing what is in them without taking the covers off, which does not look well before company. As you, William, are at the bottom of the table, and near the sideboard, if you have time you may pour out the beer, toast and water, or any thing of this kind when wanted; but I think it best for you, or any one who takes charge of the dinner, to be near the cover to see and hear the wants of the company; therefore, let the others do it. I do not mean, by what I have said, that either of you are only to do just what is allotted to you; as, for instance, you, William, would not stand to hear a person call for a thing the second time if all the rest were busy; or if the person who is on one side should see several plates want changing on the other, and none on his own side, he will not stand like a post and not help.

When you and James remove the covers from off the soup, let the others take them from you and put them in the tray, or out of the room: where there are two sorts of soups, let two of the waiters take one side to serve, the other two the other side, observing one to have one sort of soup, and the other another; this will prevent the company being teased by so many persons offering them soup if they do not choose any. When the soup is removed, put the two dishes of fish on; let two waiters hand the first round, and the other two the sauce-boats and sliced cucumber, with the cruets, if wanted: when the fish is done with, let the joints which are for top and bottom be put on : as soon as this is done, take off all the covers from the dishes; you, William, beginning at the bottom dish, and taking the left side of the table; and James beginning at the top dish, and going down the right; let this be done regularly without flurry : let those persons who take the covers from you, remove them out of the room at once; let two hand the vegetables round, the others the meat, &c. &c. Before the first course is quite done with, let the cook know, that she may be ready with the second.

You, William and James, may have a knife-tray apiece to take off the knives and forks ; begin at top and bottom, as you did in taking off the covers; or one of you may remove the knives and forks, and the other the dishes; this you must settle between you; but at this time, as there is in general enough for one to do to hand the wine about to the company, perhaps it would be as well for one to attend to this, and the other to take off the dishes, &c. while the others can take them out and fetch the rest up; if so, you, William, must remove the things from off the table, and James hand the wine. Begin, William, at the bottom dish first, to remove the knives, forks, and spoons; then go up the left side of the table, removing them as you go round, then you will leave off at the bottom; observe the same rule in taking off the dishes, and likewise in putting them on: if James helps you, let it be done as before directed, he beginning at the top,

and you at the bottom dishes: while the second
course is being brought up, you should adjust the
table, and see that there are proper carving knives
and forks, &c.

When the second course is nearly done with, let
two get different sorts of cheese and butter ready,
with salad and cucumber, or any thing which should
go on with it. Remove the second course as before
directed, when done with; then put the cheese, &c.
&c.; let two hand the cheese about, while the other
two remove the glass-coolers and wine-glasses from
off the table, as the company seldom drink wine
with their cheese. When the cheese is done with,
let it be removed, and the dirty things taken out of
the room by two, while you and the rest will clear
the table: when that is done, you, William, with a
spoon, or a brush which is for that purpose, take off
all the pieces of bread, while James follows with a
plate and clean cloth and wipes off the crumbs, and
the other two put the finger and lip glasses on;
when they are done with, put them into the trays
appointed for them; when this is done, if the
table-cloth remains on the table, you must take off
the napkins, or slips of linen cloth. If, William,
you and James go to the top of the table, one on
each side, you will be able to roll the cloth or napkins down the table to the bottom; see that there
are no crumbs of bread left on the cloth. James
and you must put the dessert and wine on, with
spoons, knives, &c. &c. while the others put the

dessert-plates and glasses round. As soon as the dessert is put on, James and you must stop to hand the ice and the wine about till the company have done eating the ice ; let the others remove every thing that is necessary to be removed from the dining-room, and begin to put the things in their proper places, and wash up the glasses, &c. &c. ; while you, William, must hold yourself in readiness to answer the dining-room bell.

If there should be cold meat on the side-table, you, William, will have to carve it ; therefore, be particular to observe the prime parts, that you may be able to serve it properly. If, in the second course, there is any thing hot, have hot plates ready, and sometimes the dish-warmers which were used for the first course will be kept on for those dishes which are served up hot in the second.

James. We are all of us much obliged to you, Sir, for your directions ; but there are still several things I should like to ask you about ; for instance, sometimes we may have a large party, with only few, in comparison, to wait on them ; sometimes, by most of the company bringing their own servants, we may have more than do us any good ; and sometimes there is great bustle and confusion occasioned by there not being a sufficient number of silver forks or spoons, or any thing else to serve the company, without having them washed, which is very inconvenient.

Onesimus. Indeed, James, I am afraid you

will often have those disagreeablenesses to complain of; therefore, before you go into the dining-room, learn who the persons are whom you have got to assist you to wait, and whether they know their business or not.

Admitting that the dinner-party should be twenty persons, and as many to wait on them, let a certain number be appointed to hand the sauce-boats round and the vegetables, while the rest shall be handing other things; be particular to settle this before the company comes into the room; let every one have his proper standing appointed him; if you do not attend to this, you will find the greater number you have to assist you, the greater will be the confusion: if you have more persons to wait on the company than six to fourteen, *only* have one besides yourself to remove and put on the table; do not suffer any other persons to do it. If you have fourteen to dinner and only four persons to wait on them, one should take off and put on the dishes, and one assist to hand the wine; you, James, should be at the bottom of the table, and the person who is to assist, at the top: let three of you hand the fish, meat, &c. &c. and one the sauces and vegetables. If you have eight to dinner, and there are only two of you to wait on them, you, James, must put on and take off the dishes, and let the other fetch up and take down the things, as you ought never to leave the room; you will not, perhaps, be able to wait on the company as you would wish, but if the person whom you have to assist you is handy in waiting, you may do a great deal if one stands at the top and the other at the bottom of the table.

As to what many servants assert, about their waiting, and managing a dinner-party, it only shows their ignorance. A person who can say that he has waited on a dozen or ten by himself, shows that he does not know what waiting at table is; for where a person has got so many to attend on, it is not properly waiting on the company, but the company *waiting for the servant*, or *serving* themselves. If you have two, or three, or more servants to assist you, and their masters or mistresses sit near together, you must not let them stand behind them, but appoint them in their proper places, according to the directions I have before given to William and you, and I have no doubt but you will then be able to go through the dinner comfortably: if the servants should say it is their master's or mistress's wish that they should stand behind them when dining out, you may observe to them, that they can tell them the reason why they did not; for, suppose the room should be particularly narrow just in the place where one is to stand, this would perhaps be the cause of much confusion if not of accidents. Always choose the persons who know most of waiting at table to hand the plates round; let the others take the sauce and vegetables; or if any are very awkward, let them stand near the plate-basket and take the plates out of the person's hand who brings them, and put them therein, and put the clean ones ready with the knife and fork in it; and always before any strange servants go in to wait at table, take them first and show them the room, and where the different things are put, and how it is to be conducted, and if there are any particular ways in which any thing is to be served up, or any of the company require any thing particular, it ought to be explained.

As to not having enough plate for the dinner without washing, I must acknowledge this has often been the cause of much confusion in the dining-room; to rectify it, have a jug of hot water and one of cold just at the outside of the dining-room door, or some place near at hand, and if you can arrange with one of the maids to wash them for you, it will be all the better; if not, do as before, as you can wash them in the time you would be running up and down stairs to do it; if you should not have plates sufficient, recollect it in time to send some down to the cook to have them washed ready.

AN EVENING PARTY, OR ROUT.

Onesimus. Now, William, I shall observe to you a few things concerning an evening party, or *rout.* I have before advised you, when the dinner was over

2

to see about tea and coffee, and the lighting up of the drawing-rooms; let the rest wash up, and put their things in their proper places to be ready against the time the evening company comes. The ladies in general leave the dining-room before the gentlemen, and have coffee first, the gentlemen often have it carried to them there. You ought to take up both the coffee and tea if you possibly can, or have persons to assist you who know the company, and are able to hand the tea and coffee, according to the priority of rank in the company. When the gentlemen leave the dining-room you should go in the first and put away the wine. If it so happens that you are taking up tea or coffee, you should turn the key of the door, and not suffer any person to go in, as it too often happens that persons who are assisting to wait at table will go into the room when the butler is not present, and drink and lavish the wine away with the dessert; indeed I have known a table entirely stripped of the remains of the fruit, &c. &c. and a great deal of wine drank; this is truly distressing to the person who is answerable for the care of those things, therefore if you cannot attend to it when the gentlemen leave the dining-room, lock the door and put the key in your pocket till you can. When servants and waiters are waiting at dinner, it is however customary that they should live well and have plenty of good beer; that is, enough to do them good, and where they have

not this they will in general take every opportunity
of stealing whatever they can lay their hands on in
the eating and drinking way, which is not to be
wondered at; therefore, when you have company,
always try to make the persons who help to wait
comfortable, by getting necessary things for them,
which I am sure no reasonable master or mistress
will deny, if properly spoken to about it. But you
must not suppose, that you are to drink your master's
and mistress's wine, and lavish it away as you would
small beer : there are many ladies and gentlemen
who would not mind their servants having a glass of
wine on such occasions as those, if they did not take
more; but such is the unfaithfulness of servants, that
they will absolutely waste it, and sometimes even get
drunk, so as not to be able to wait on the company.
Thus one evil brings on another. I think myself
a little good beer is the best for servants ; but if your
master or mistress ask you to have a glass of wine,
always accept it ; if you cannot drink it then, there
may be a time you can, or some of your fellow-
servants may be glad of it; but when you are
intrusted with the wine, neither make away with it,
nor let your mind hanker after it, but endeavour to
fulfil your trust with uprightness, doing to your
master what you would wish a servant to do to you,
if you were in your master's situation. In taking the
dessert things away, be careful not to knock the
dishes and plates about, so as to chip or break them.

Let the wine and other things be put in their proper places; do not let them stand to tempt persons. Let all the napkins be folded up, and the chairs set round the sides of the room the first thing, that you may not run against them, and break what things you may have in your hands; let the glasses be removed into the pantry, and every thing put in its proper place.

TEA AND COFFEE.

You, William and James, I shall suppose to take up the tea and coffee. With the coffee there is seldom any thing eaten, therefore one is sufficient to take it; but the tea in general has some eatables with it, such as plum-cake, toast, or bread and butter: therefore one of you must take the tea, and the other the eatables, and hand their tray to the company, holding it as handy and conveniently as you can for them to help themselves. The one who takes up the eatables should wait in the room to receive the cups and saucers in the tray from the company, for it too often happens that they set their cups and glasses on the mantlepiece, tables, and other places, which often get stained by them, particularly by the ice-glasses. Be exact in having the refreshments up in proper time according to your orders, as I have known a great number of the company leave before they have been served, through the inattention of the servant, in this respect; therefore be always rather before your time than after it.

ANNOUNCING NAMES.

When you expect the company, you ought all to be in your proper places ready to receive them. I shall consider that there are six of you; two to take up the refreshments, and the other four to show up the visitors; let one person be at the drawing-room door to announce the names to the lady or gentleman who stands there to receive them; let another stand at the bottom of the staircase to announce them to the one who stands at the drawing-room door, and the one who opens the street-door must announce them to the one who stands at the bottom of the staircase; let the other one stand in the hall, but not attempt to announce, for it too often happens, the more persons are in the hall to receive the company, the greater the confusion is, for they perplex each other. If there are six or ten persons to receive the company, only have three to announce the names, unless the hall and staircase should be very long; and the persons who are to give the names up should be well acquainted with the company; all the servants must, however, stand in the hall that can be spared, for *show*, particularly the livery servants. If the person who gives up the names thoroughly understands them, this will prevent mistakes. It often happens, when one family have been announced as coming in, that their names have been given up to the person at the drawing-room door, while they may have gone into a room to take off their cloaks or shawls, and adjust their dress, and others have come in and gone up before them; this has caused great confusion, particularly if the waiter who stands at the drawing-room door do not know the company personally: in this case the person who stands at the bottom of the staircase must be on the look-out, and if any who go in there stay long and others come during the time, he must not give up the names of those who are gone into the room, till they come out again. If any ladies or gentlemen stay there for some time, and the person who stands at the bottom of the staircase has forgotten their names, which is often the case, he ought to ask them again, and not let them go up stairs without announcing them to the person who stands at the drawing-room door. Be very particular to have each servant in his proper place, and keep him in it. You would do well to have a list of all the names of the visitors, and look it over now and then, and read them aloud; this, with paying attention in the morning visits, how the servants pronounce the names, would be a great assistance to you at such times, as you should endeavour to have a right pronunciation of them, without which you will often make mistakes. If at any time the strange servants in the hall who are waiting for their families make a noise, or any remarks on the company coming in, you must forbid it; if they do not desist, you must turn them out. It is too often the case that servants forget themselves on those occasions, and will be laughing and making their remarks, which is highly improper, and often complained of. You must see also that they do not obstruct the company in coming in and going out in the hall, by putting their legs across it; it is through the ill conduct of servants, that many ladies and gentlemen will not suffer any to come into the hall; and it is truly distressing, for poor servants whose health is not very good, to stand out all weathers in the cold and damp, and wait perhaps for hours. If you can have seats for servants, always try for it, but make them in return keep quiet. You must observe the same rule when the company are leaving the house, as you did at their coming in: the person who stands at the drawing-room door must announce the names as they come down, to the person who stands at the bottom of the staircase, for him to call the servant who is waiting, that he may have the carriage up ready; if he is not in the hall, let the person who stands to open the street-door call aloud for the servant, but he ought not to go further, as every one should be at his post when the company are going out, and the servants who come for their families ought to be within call.

When you have a large party or *rout*, intercede for a constable to keep order among the coachmen : this is highly necessary for the comfort of the company in setting down and taking up, particularly if the weather be wet; and not only this, but out of humanity to the poor horses, as they are often cut and beaten shockingly at such times: this is a piece of unnecessary cruelty towards those useful animals, which calls aloud for the interference of ladies and gentlemen of humanity to have some effectual means brought forward which shall do it away. it is often done in trying to break the rank. If there be a constable, and he makes the coachman set down *one way* and take up *another*, and keep in the *rank*, this will prevent confusion, and the company will be able to get in and out of their carriages faster and without risk; as accidents often occur when there is no person properly to regulate them.

SUPPER.

William. I thank you, Sir, for these observations, and I have no doubt but we all shall receive benefit by them; but it sometimes happens that at those parties many of the ladies and gentlemen stop supper, and have it in the drawing-room, so that we cannot get the cloth laid till the others are gone, in fact till it is ordered.

Onesimus. I shall first give Joseph directions

how to set out a supper-table, and I will then make a few observations to you on having supper in the drawing-room.

I shall consider, Joseph, that the company you have in the evening make up but a small party, that is, about twenty or thirty to supper. Such parties as those are very common in small families where there is only one servant kept, and they seldom have company to dinner when they have a supper party. In those small parties the company in general play at card, therefore observe to have all your lamps and candles lighted up in the drawing-room a little before they come. If there is a glass chandelier or sconces, and if they are so high that you cannot reach them without steps, you had better have a small cane or stick with a wax-taper tied at the end, and an extinguisher; if you have this, you will be enabled to light them and put them out without having to bring the steps into the room, which is very inconvenient at such times: always prepare your candles before you set them up, that they may be ready to light without much trouble. I hope you never will attempt to blow them out, when the company are gone, with your *mouth*, or even a pair of *bellows*, as this is both dirty and very dangerous. Have your tea-things in readiness, with every thing belonging thereto, and likewise the glasses, &c. for the refreshments, which in general are carried up to the company in the drawing-room before they have supper: let this be so ordered and arranged, that you can have it when wanted without confusion. If the weather be cold, make up good fires in the rooms, and let the hearth be well swept before the company come, also the card-tables set, the chairs adjusted, and every thing properly arranged.

THE SUPPER-TABLE.

You can always lay your table-cloth for supper before the company comes, if the room is not made use of to make the tea or prepare the refreshments in. You ought to know what number of visitants are expected; then place the chairs close to one another; this will be a rule to guide you what length the table should be. In putting the linen cloth on, be as particular as at dinner. Put one knife and fork to each person, unless you are short of waiters; in this case put two. Let your carving knives and forks, salts and spoons, be put as at dinner, and a wine-glass to the right of each person, about four inches from the edge of the table. Glass-coolers, finger-glasses, or napkins, are very seldom used for supper. You must have proper water decanters, or jugs, to set on the table with spring-water in them. Let two or three glasses be put for each of the company, as they in general help themselves. If it is a cold supper, you can put a plate for each person round; but if there should be any thing hot, you must have hot plates; this is, however, seldom the case in small families. You can set your supper things on the table before the supper is ordered, therefore you may take your time in putting it on ; you will have a bill of fare to direct you. Be particular to have the dishes put on the table as it is there directed, as every dish is contrived to answer each other ; let the dishes be put in a proper line and at equal distances from each other, and the edges and ends of the table. There is seldom any changing of dishes at a supper-table in a small family, particularly if cold ; it is generally all on at once, therefore you will not want so many things as at dinner ; but have plenty of rummers and tumbler-glasses. Let your side-board and side-table and every thing be set out as at dinner. The decanters of wine are in general put on the supper-table : observe the same rule here as at dinner ; if there are only pint decanters on the supper-table, it will be necessary to have more than if they were quart ones ; but this depends on your employers, and they will give you directions accordingly. Study, however, to put on every thing, so that it may look handsome, and as though you had a design in setting it out. In general, the dishes which are sent up for supper, the meat as well as the fruit, are garnished with various green leaves and flowers ; be particular not to shake them off in carrying them up, as they give the supper-table a pretty appearance.

In waiting, observe the same rule which I gave to William at dinner, and be regulated according to the number of persons you have to assist; let every one have his proper place appointed, and what to do.

SUPPER IN THE DRAWING-ROOM.

I shall now, William, observe a few things to you concerning the company having supper in the drawing-room: this often causes great confusion, as it is always done in a hurry; and very often the tables from the dining-room are to be carried up into the drawing-room for supper; if you have this to do, be careful that you do not knock the corners against the wall in coming up. Let your glasses, knives, forks, plates, and every thing be in readiness, and likewise the supper all got ready in good time, that you may have nothing to do, but just to set the table and put the things on when you have got the orders; in fact, you should so place your things below, that you will have nothing to do but merely to take them into the room when called for. Have a green cloth, or piece of carpet, to put under your plate-basket and knife-trays, as, in a hurry, things may be slopped or spilt out of the plates, which would spoil the carpet. Have your tray-stands in the room to put your various things on in the trays, as you will have no sideboard; if there be a drugget, instead of a carpet, which the drawing-room floor is covered with, you must be doubly on your guard, and never put the dishes or plates thereon. When the supper is served up in this way, there is not so much form as when it is laid out in the rooms below; but always arrange it in the best way you can. When supper is over, and the company gone, look up your plate, and see that it is all right; because, if not, the present will be the time to look after it, as it sometimes happens that spoons, forks, &c. are thrown into the dust-hole, or hog-tub, with bits and scraps, therefore always count it up the same night or the next morning. Let the lights in the drawing-room and parlour be put out with the extinguisher, as before directed; let the lamps be turned down, not blown out; let the thing which is to keep up the oil in the lamp be put up when you put it out, this will prevent the oil from over-flowing, which it is apt to do when it is warm.

I think I have now said sufficient to give you an insight into the manner and ways of setting out the tables and properly waiting on a small party; and although in a few things there may be a trifling difference in some families, still the foregoing observations will be of service to all, if you properly attend to them.

THE KITCHEN MEALS.

And now, my young friends, having taught you how to attend on the meals of your superiors, I will give you a little advice as to the proper mode of conducting yourselves at your own. In all families there is, or ought to be, a set time for the servants to have their meals, when all should endeavour to attend, as, without this, it will be impossible to go on comfortably; you must therefore arrange your work so as not to be loitering about when you should be at your meals, as the manner of some is, which often is the cause of sad contention and confusion; for, if one servant comes at one time and another at another, it interferes with the cook and her work, so that she will not be able to do her business regularly; besides, how unthankful and irreverent it is not to be round the table, when a blessing is asked on the bounties which the good hand of the Lord has provided for the returning wants and necessities of our bodily health, which we ought to receive with thankfulness, and acknowledge by our attention to the set times appointed for it, our good behaviour while receiving it, and our readiness in returning to our proper occupations afterwards. Let us not be like some we read of, who *ate* and *drank*, and then *rose up to play;* but let us receive our provisions thankfully and eat moderately, and not meet at the dinner-table, or any other, to quarrel and dispute with each other, which too often is the case, and to complain of the cooking, or the provisions not being good enough: this is what I have often seen in persons who had scarcely ever known the comfort and pleasure of eating a good meal before they entered gentlemen's service. How wicked is such conduct toward God, who has made their cup to run over in natural things; and how ungrateful to their employers, who provide bountifully to make them comfortable and happy! In some families they are very strict, and will not wait for any servant; if they do not attend at the time appointed, the provisions are removed from the table and put away, and this is what ought to be in every family. If any of the servants be kept from their meals by particular business of their employers, it is a different case, there should then be a sufficient portion cut comfortably off, and put by for them; for the whole ought not to be kept waiting for one, unless it is ordered to the contrary. It is the rule in some families that the man or boy should lay the cloth for the servants; it is always the boy's place to do it where there are both kept, therefore lay it in time for the cook to put the dinner on at the appointed hour. The man-servants likewise always have to draw the beer for dinner or supper; never draw too much at once, but rather go twice than run the risk of wasting it. If there be too much accidentally drawn at any time, put it into a bottle, and keep it for the next time you draw, and mix it with the fresh: shameful waste often brings woful want to those who are so sinful as to be careless and extravagant in the provisions committed to their charge. Be clean and tidy at meal-times, and talk but little while eating; I have known some who have been so rude as to talk all manner of filthy conversation at such times, which is a disgrace to any human being, and ought not to be suffered in any place, above all in a gentleman's house. Some likewise cannot sit a moment without lolling upon the table, or cutting and chipping a bit of bread, or something of that kind, or rubbing the table-cloth with their fingers, or else knocking the knives against each other: avoid all such foolish actions. If you have done eating first, sit upright and behave respectfully, and never get up till all have done, unless your business calls you. Do not abuse the plenty you may see before you by suffering it to tempt you to eat and drink till you can do it no longer, or till you feel uncomfortable: this is a *hoggish* practice, and frustrates the designs of Providence; for, when the stomach is overcharged, it does harm instead of good, as it cannot digest well, particularly if you have not much exercise, as you cannot then require so much support; and gluttony and excess not only unfit the body for exercise, but likewise clog the wheels of the mind, and make it seem a trouble to read, move, think, or do any thing else. When you have done dinner put your chair back in its proper place, and never leave your things about for others to wait on you, as you must consider there is no servant kept to wait on another; therefore, always help to clear away the things and put them into their proper places. If at any time you should see your fellow-servants busy and not able to come at the hour appointed for meals, lend them a hand if you can, so that you may, if possible, be all together at those times; this will be acting like a Christian; for, how heathenish it is to see a family of servants come to meals, one at one time and another at another, without asking a blessing on what the LORD in HIS goodness has provided, or returning thanks for what has been received? this is done in too many families, but we are ordered by the LORD to receive every thing with thanksgiving and prayer, and in so doing you will have such comfort and blessing in receiving, as the drunkard and gluttonous man can never know.

BEHAVIOUR TO YOUR FELLOW-SERVANTS.

MUCH of the comfort of servants depends on their behaviour and conduct towards each other;

H 3

and you will always find, the more you endeavour to promote the happiness of those around you, the more you will secure your own. Consider that you must live with fellow-servants like yourself, made up of imperfections, which will give you an opportunity of exercising your patience and forbearance towards them, as they will have to do towards you.

Be not hasty in passing judgment on any one, as we are called on to act with Christian charity towards each other; that is, to do unto others as we would they should do unto us, were we in their situation and they in ours: if this were to be attended to, our lives would pass more pleasantly with us than they do; but how different is the practice in general to this I have no need to say, as observation and woful experience will soon teach us what domestic quarrels families are too often the scenes of. There you will see *envy, malice, duplicity, dishonesty, misrepresentation,* and every other evil, to the tormenting of each other, instead of dwelling together in affection and unity, and living in peace and happiness, and making their home a little heaven, as they might if they were so inclined; instead of which they make it a *hell* on earth, by their wicked ways and disagreeable tempers, and wishing to tyrannize over each other: this seems to be the great *bane* in families, as I have known places where the servants have had every necessary good to make them comfortable provided by their employers, yet are miserable and wretched through not agreeing one with the other; thinking, I suppose, that happiness and respectability consist in having rule and authority over our fellow-servants; but this is quite a mistake, as it consists in performing the duty which is allotted us, and doing unto others as we would wish they should do unto us: herein lies our *true happiness*.

One great source of contention and confusion among servants is one waiting for another to do what he ought to do himself. Therefore know your work and do it; but if it should so happen that you have not time, ask your fellow-servants with civility to do it for you, or to help you, and be always ready to lend them a hand to do any thing in return, or if they should have forgotten any thing, to do it for them, if they are not in the way to do it themselves.

When any of your fellow-servants or any other person tells you tales about others, be not hasty in crediting what they say, but observe in what way they represent it, and whether they try to make the most of it, or not; try also to find out whether they have had any quarrel with the persons they are speaking of, and whether they seem to triumph over any of their failings; or bargain that their own name must not be mentioned; if so, you may rely on it, that a great deal, if not all, of

what they say is false. Keep such persons always
at a distance from you, treat them civilly, but have
nothing to do with them any further than your
business calls you.

It is the lot of all Adam's race to be born to
afflictions; servants, therefore, have it more or less
as well as others, and at such times we are called
upon to exercise our religious charity; and the more
readily to assist each other in cases of illness,
as we know not how soon it may be our lot to be
laid on a bed of sickness ourselves. I have known
the good intentions of a benevolent master and mistress towards an afflicted servant often frustrated
through the ill-nature of the rest of the servants,
who would not do any thing for them; thus, the
poor afflicted creatures have been sent out of the
house through the *cruelty* of their own companions. Such persons would do well to consider the
words of our blessed Lord and Saviour Jesus
Christ, as recorded in Matt. chap. vii. ver. 2, " *With
what measure ye mete to others it shall be measured
out to you again;* " and many more of like import;
but let this suffice. Now consider, my young friends,
how distressing must be the feelings of servants
when ill and not able to do their work ; but how
much more must they feel when under the necessity
of being removed out of their place through the ill-
nature of their fellow-servants, perhaps having no
where to go to; no friends, and but little money to

support them: this ought deeply to impress our minds, and fill us with a desire to alleviate the distresses of those who are afflicted, and to do as much of their work, and wait on them, as far as in us lies. Never let us add to the sorrow of persons in affliction by our cruelty and uncouthness, but rather let us do all in our power to comfort them and alleviate their sufferings, even if they have treated us ill before; let us forget it all when affliction overtakes them, and try to win them to love and respect us by our kindness and attention to them when they cannot help themselves. These are the principles which will bring true peace to the mind if practised, and which have been the means to soften and melt a person into contrition who, perhaps, may have shown but just before a stubborn and disagreeable temper. How blessed is such revenge as this, which can soften the bitterness and cold-heartedness of our enemies, and win them to love us, rather than render evil for evil!

Never irritate a person of a contentious spirit, nor hold any argument with such an one. Wherever you may live, try to please all and live in peace with all; make as many friends as you can, and as few enemies; watch over your own temper and conduct with scrupulosity; try not to provoke any one, not even a foolish or conceited person, for, if you reprove such, they will hate you, when a wise person would love and respect you. Watch over the failings of others, as warnings to yourself; and always try to do unto others as you would wish they should do unto you were you in their situation; keep this in mind, and you will find it support you under every vexation and trial, and prevent you from many hasty actions and words, and many an evil deed which you might fall into if not checked by such considerations. By curbing the first breaking out of our temper, and keeping a watchful eye over our actions, we shall soon gain such command over ourselves as will add much to our own comfort as well as the comfort of those about us; but if we do not practise constant watchfulness, we shall make but small progress in this amiable and peaceful state of mind.

Be not hasty in running up to your master or mistress with the faults of your fellow-servants; when they do wrong admonish them, and if they will not hear you, state to them the consequence of their conduct, and how it will hurt their character if they do not mind how they behave themselves : but if at any time they should do any thing that you find it necessary to let your master or mistress know, do not make the most of it, and still less make it worse than it really is; but state it in as simple a manner as possible, not with a deep designing insinuation against the unfortunate offenders. Consider what injury you do to their character, and how easily they may be thrown out of bread by it, and perhaps led on to greater evils. Let no mistaken zeal for your employers tempt you thus into irritating them, by magnifying the faults of any one that may serve them; and, above all, guard against being influenced in so doing by an envious, lying, or revengeful spirit. Remember that "*the Lord abhors the deceitful man, and will not let him go unpunished.*" SOLOMON says, "*He that uttereth a slander is a fool.*" And when we recollect that a servant depends on his character for his bread, how careful ought we to be of what we say of each other!

If any of your fellow-servants should have the misfortune to be deformed, or have any blemish or defect in their person, do not make them the objects of your derision: such conduct is shocking to the highest degree, though too frequent among idle ignorant people. It is affliction enough to the unfortunate persons to have to bear about them inconveniencies which often stand in the way of their getting their bread; and we ought always to keep in mind that we are none of us our own makers, nor can we make one hair on our head *white* or *black*, or add one cubit to our stature; thus our dear LORD tells us: then what an abuse of our reasonable faculties must it be, when we suffer ourselves to mock a fellow-creature; and what presumption, insult, and ingratitude must it be to our Maker, to reproach and insult those to whom he has not thought fit to be so liberal in outward appearance as he has been to us. No, my young friends; let us show our gratitude and thankfulness to our benevolent Creator by our good behaviour, and our desire to promote the happiness of those whom he has not so much favoured in the eyes of men; but to whom he may nevertheless have granted inward tranquillity and spiritual graces, far transcending any other good. Another fault, nearly akin to that which I have been treating of, and indeed I scarcely know which is the worst of the two, is ill-treating any poor servant who may not be so well off, or have such respectable friends as ourselves. I have often been grieved to see how shamefully some poor fatherless and motherless young persons have been behaved to by their fellow-servants, who have shown by such conduct a most wicked, nay, devilish disposition. What! my young friends, shall we *provoke*, *oppress*, *ill-treat*, and *tyrannize* over those who are not able to *defend themselves?* God forbid! rather let us do all we can to help them on their way, that it may not appear to them so rugged and forlorn. Consider what they must feel, when ill treated, to have no person to open their mind to, perhaps no brother, or sister, or friend near them to sympathize with them or console them ; no parental care or advice to guide them in the best way; but cast into the world to seek their bread under many difficulties and disadvantages which others know not. O my young friends, you, who have relations to sympathize with you, still think it hard when you are ill treated ; how much more then must those feel it who have no relations or friends? I hope each of you will do all in your power to befriend and sympathize with the fatherless or motherless, or those who are still worse off, in having parents that set them a bad example by their own wicked conduct. Never re-proach those persons with the conduct of their relations, as they perhaps are already too much grieved and ashamed of it. If you live with aged persons, treat them respectfully, and never reflect on them because they may be old, as many young persons are too apt to do. Consider how you would feel if you were old and not able to do your work as you were used to do, and then to be upbraided by a young ignorant servant, who scarcely knows any thing but impertinence. Persons when they get old have often enough to put up with from hard-hearted employers, and the in-firmity of their own years, without the upbraidings of the young; besides, you may live to old age yourself, and, through various divine providences, you may be under the necessity of remaining in service at a time when you had hoped to have a fireside of your own. If it be through their own improvidence, or improper conduct, they are under the necessity of continuing in servitude to get their

1

bread, they do not deserve so much pity and sympathy; but still be not severe on their failings, as you, also, are in the body subject to the like passions; always, therefore, respect the aged, and defend the fatherless and motherless child and those who have no friend: never oppress them, for, if you do, God will arise up for them ere long, and vindicate their cause, to the confusion of their oppressors. Read what he hath said by his servants: David saith, that " *God shall break in pieces the oppressor*," Psalm lxxii.; and in the 12th he saith, " *For the oppression of the poor and the sighing of the needy, now will I arise, saith the Lord; I will set him in safety from him that puffeth at him.*" If the Lord is on the side of the fatherless and motherless, and with the poor and the needy, which he certainly is, and makes their cause his cause, which you may see that he does if you read Psalm x. ver. 14, 18; Psalm lxviii. ver. 5; Malachi, chap. iii. ver. 5; may we not ask, Who ever fought against the Lord and prospered? The answer is ready—NONE. How much better will it be to act and do as holy Job did, both for our own comfort and those round about us! Hear what the good man saith in chap. xxxix. " *I was eyes to the blind, and feet was I to the lame; I was a father to the poor; and the cause which I knew not I searched out; and I brake the jaws of the wicked, and plucked the spoil out of his teeth.*" I say unto each of you, go, and do ye likewise, as far as it is in your power so to do.

When any of your fellow-servants get promoted, or have any presents made them for their good behaviour, do not be dissatisfied and envious of them; but let it stimulate you to greater attention, that you may receive the same mark of respect at some future period. Behave to your fellow-servants who may be in authority over you, with every deference due to their situation; receive their commands respectfully and obey them cheerfully, as they are only set over you to see that things are kept in proper order; therefore receive their *corrections* and *admonitions* with thankfulness, as by so doing they will find it pleasant to instruct you, and you will gain useful knowledge by your humility; besides, it is our duty to behave respectfully to those who are in authority over us, for, if you should live in service a number of years, you would not like to be insulted by a boy or a girl just taken into a family, therefore do as you would be done by; and if you have to deliver your employer's commands to your fellow-servants at any time, whether they be under you or not, do. not speak in an austere or domineering manner, and make a pompous use of that little pronoun *I ;* but deliver them as coming from your master or mistress, and never usurp authority over any of your fellow-servants. As some which I know, through their pride, ignorance, and domineering manner are hated wherever they go, I therefore again exhort you to observe the golden rule, " *so do unto others as you would wish they*

*should do unto you, were you in their situation
and they in yours;*" this will be a sure rule and
guide to all of you, and lead you in the path of
earthly peace to eternal happiness.

DRESS.

It forms an important part of an in-door servant's
business to keep himself clean and well dressed;
indeed it is thought so much of by some families,
that they will not take a person into their house
who has not a smart and clean appearance. Every
servant, therefore, ought to be allowed money and
clothes sufficient to do it with; but he must not
bestow so much time or thought on his person as
to divert his attention from his work. I have
known some, whose appearance has given the
greatest satisfaction, yet who were so slovenly in
their business that their employers were forced to
discharge them; and others, who have done their
work admirably, yet so far neglected cleanliness in
their own person, that they were obliged to be
discharged also. It is only by uniting cleanliness
and neatness of person with assiduity and attention
in your business, that you will make a good servant.

Recollect, however, respectability does not consist in having a large gold chain and bunch of
seals, or in our cravats being tied on so tight that
we cannot move our heads without turning the whole

body, nor even in letting a pocket-handkerchief hang out of the pocket a foot long; nor does it consist in wearing clothes which are too expensive for the situation we are in, although we may ape the *dandy*, and strut about like persons of consequence, and treat our fellow-servants as though they were not worthy of our notice: all this will not make us respectable servants. I shall, therefore, endeavour to point out to you wherein I consider true respectability to consist, as I not only wish you all to be good servants, but that your conduct may be an honour to your employers, and a credit to that part of the community you are in, as well as a benefit to society.

In the first place, you must consider, that when you go out to service you must dress to please others rather than yourself; steer clear of either a slovenly habit, or a foppish and extravagant one; the two rocks upon which weak and vain minds are apt to split. Take heed that what you wear may be becoming the situation you are in, and never try to outvie your master in dress. I have seen this done, and I have also seen the same servants afterwards like vagrants when they have been out of place for even a little while, having spent in extravagance and folly what they ought to have saved for their support in the time of necessity and affliction. You should have proper things for changing, enough to last a fortnight without washing, particularly if you have to travel. Let your shirts have frills to them ; have white cotton stockings and white cravats to wait on the family, and never wear black or any coloured neckcloths after the morning, as they do not look respectable for a servant: you can, however, have coloured stockings and neckcloths to do your dirty work in. If you have a livery found you, of course you will have sufficient to appear clean and creditable in, with hats and wash-leather gloves; but if you find your own clothes, let them be made well, and of good quality, but never in the extreme of the fashion. Tie your neckcloth neatly, and use a stiffener in it ; turn your hair up in front, and let the other part be kept smooth. If you have to wear hair-powder, be very particular in keeping your hair in order, and in adjusting it again when rumpled, as the respectability of a servant's appearance greatly depends on his hair being in order, and his neckcloth neatly tied. Never put your stockings on with holes in them, as they make a wretched contrast to a fine coat. Be particular in having your linen well washed, as it often happens that servants' things are neglected. Never wear them too long, or make them too dirty before you have them washed. Always have drawers instead of linings to your small-clothes, that you may have them washed; likewise keep your feet clean, and often change your stockings, particularly in the summer, if your feet be damp, for, if you do not, they will be very disagreeable to persons about you;

but you must not soak them much in water, for this will make them very tender : keep a towel for this purpose, and dip it into water, and rub a little soap on, and wipe them every day, or as often as you change your stockings, which must be once if not twice in a day. Keep your person clean altogether, and change your linen frequently.

You will find it necessary to have two day shirts in a week, besides a night one to do your dirty work in ; and at least four pair of stockings a week, or perhaps one a day. In some places you will be obliged to wear silk stockings, but in such cases the family find them ; never buy any yourself. If at any time you have not proper things for change, ask your employers to advance you a little money, to buy you a few necessary things, rather than go shabby and dirty; and never think of taking an unlawful step to get any thing, as I have known some do, and be heartily sorry for it when it was too late. You will find it necessary to have several pairs of shoes, as you will want thick ones for the carriage and to walk about in, and light ones to wait at table in. You ought not to wear boots unless you are travelling; nor ought you to wait at table in gaiters; but in some families the servants are kept on the run till the last moment; in this case you will find it necessary to keep your gaiters on, as they will look much better than dirty stockings: if you have time, always change your things, and wash yourself, be-

fore dinner; but in some families you will find it
impossible to do so, as they are unthinking enough
to keep the servant out till the dinner is ordered,
and ready to be put on the table. If you find this
the case, let it make you more on the alert in having
your things all laid out ready, so that if you can
find a moment, you may slip them on without loss
of time, as it is particularly desirable to appear neat
and clean in waiting at dinner.

You will find it impossible to do well without a
watch, as you will often be ordered at a particular
time, when you perhaps may not be able to get to
look at a clock; besides which, clocks frequently differ, and a few minutes are at some times of particular
consequence. You therefore must have a watch,
if you wish to be a good and attentive servant.
But there is no occasion to go to an extravagant
price for one; be more particular to get a good one,
that will keep time well, than a fine-looking one
with a great bunch of seals; as that is foppish and
extravagant, and we may all find better uses for
our money than merely to nurse our pride with it.

If you take a place where you are to find your
own clothes, and are expected to wear a livery, you
must well consider before you buy your cloth,
whether the place suits you, or you suit the family,
or whether they are often changing their servants;
for, if you have livery suits made up for a family,
and you should not be able to stay, they will
be of little use to you afterwards; for you cannot

wear them in another place, and you will get
scarcely any thing for them, although they may be
nearly new. When you find yourself livery, let it be
good, and if you stop some years in a family you will
be able to save by it ; as it often happens that tailors
will make up any kind of cloth for servants, thinking they have no voice to speak ; thus their clothes
are shabby in a very little time ; but if you find
it yourself, you can have much better cloth for
the same money. You should likewise have a plain
suit of clothes by you to put on occasionally when
you may want to go out to spend a day ; besides, service is no inheritance, and you may want
in a hurry, and if you should not have any by you,
you will be placed in an awkward situation ; but
let it be neat : and observe the same rule if you find
plain clothes for yourself instead of a livery ; never
have your things made in a dandy shape and manner. I have seen servants, and particularly valets
and butlers, who have just got into place, dress in
so unbecoming a manner, as if they meant to out-
shine the gentlemen they served, that they have re-
minded me of the frog in the fable, who would swell
itself out to vie with the ox ; and, like the poor
frog, they have generally been ruined in the foolishness of their endeavour : let such examples be warnings to us not to do the same.

BEHAVIOUR.

THE next thing which presents itself to view, after our *dress*, is our *address* and behaviour to those whom we serve, and those round about us; for, what good clothes are to the body, to set it off and make it appear respectable, civility and modesty are to the mind; fitting us for sociability in society, and making us move with honour and respectability in the sphere of life in which the kind hand of Providence has placed us: therefore, I would wish you, my young friends, to pay particular attention to what I say on this subject, as, without good behaviour, your road through life will be rough and thorny, and often cause you to lie down in sorrow at night, when, if you had acted with discretion and kindness, you might have moved on with smoothness and enjoyed sweet repose.

In the first place, whenever your master or mistress calls to you, or speaks to you, never say *Yes*, or *No*, merely; but, YES, SIR; or, No, MA'AM: or if it should be a lady or gentleman of title, let them be addressed according to the title they bear; as, *Yes, my Lord;* or, *No, my Lord: Yes, my Lady*; or, *No, my Lady.* If you live where there are a housekeeper and butler, you must answer them, *Yes, Sir*, and *Yes, Ma'am;* as this is a mark of respect due to them in their situation, and ought to be paid to them. Never offer to talk, or force a conversation with your master or mistress, or any branch of the family; for, to do so is impertinence which will not be easily looked over by many: nor make yourself familiar with any of the younger branches of the family, as many disagreeablenesses have arisen from so doing; but keep yourself at a respectful distance; and be ready to give an answer when asked about any thing, in as few words as you possibly can, and with modesty and reverence, not with ostentatiousness and parade; if you do not know the particulars you are asked about, be honest, and say so; and do not endeavour to deceive those who ask you, by pretending to know what you really do not.

If you ever hear the family, or any visitor, talking, or arguing upon any subject whatever, even if you know it, and they may be both in the dark, still you have no business to notice it, although you could set them right in one moment: but if they should condescend to ask you about it, reply as before directed; but never make use of such words as these, when asked;—*You are right, Sir*, or *Ma'am*; or, *This gentleman is right, and the other is wrong*: for, whenever you are asked a question, you must consider that you are not expected to argue and dispute about it, but merely to state what you know, with simplicity and impartiality, taking no part on either side; which is all that is required of you.

If those with whom you live ever conde-scend to ask you how any thing is done, or which is the best way to do it, give your opinion in a modest manner, as before directed; but if they should after all take their own way, and that prove to be wrong, you must not notice it, or say if they should condescend to ask your opinion another time, that it is of no use to give it, as they will not take it, although you told them the right way before; for this would be assuming a consequence which does not become a servant, let him be high or low in situation.

Should a master or mistress think proper to admonish you for any fault, or supposed fault, do not answer with impertinence; if you are wrong, take care that you do not the same thing again; but if not, take it patiently, and never reply in passion: re-fute an unjust charge coolly, if you have an oppor-tunity, but if they will not suffer you to prove your innocence, fret not yourself; perhaps they may see in a little while that you were innocent of what they laid to your charge; if not, it is better to suffer innocently than justly for our faults.

Whenever you receive messages or commands from those whom you serve, or indeed from any lady or gentleman, do not turn your head another way while they are speaking to you, but look at them, not with a bold stare, but with a modest and steady countenance.

If you gain the confidence and approbation of those whom you serve, and get favour through it, do not be vain and high-minded, nor proud and insolent towards your fellow-servants, or assume a haughtiness towards your employers, and fancy they cannot do without you, because you are a valuable servant to them. Nothing can show more ignorance, wickedness, and vanity in a person, than, when he is promoted himself, to ill-treat his fellow-servants, and to behave with impertinence towards his benefactors: show your gratitude rather by an increase of attention and assiduity to your benefactors, and by doing all you can for your fellow-servants to bring them forward in the same manner; by which conduct your own happiness will be increased. Never indulge the *abominable* and *hateful* spirit to wish to get into favour by aspersing and calumniating your fellow-servants, which is too much the case, now-a-days, to the distraction of the family peace, and curse of all the rest of the servants. It cannot be good behaviour towards our employers to keep tormenting and irritating their temper with dark insinuations about the rest of the servants: always consider the less you vex them, either yourself, or on account of others, the better servant you will be to them.

Always show your respect to the family by *moving your hat* when you meet any of them; never keep it on in the house, or sit down in the presence of your master or mistress, unless they

I

bid you. Never make a noise or talk loud in the house. Keep from singing, bawling, and whistling; this may do in the country to frighten the birds from the field, but not for a gentleman's house; here you must endeavour to go about as still as you possibly can, and do your work *quietly and quickly.*

There are various ways wherein you can show your respect and attention to your superiors; therefore, make it your *study how to please:* this will add both to your profit and likewise to your comfort; as in gentlemen's service there will be times and seasons when you will see things, and are not to see them; when you will hear things, and are not to hear them; when you will know things, and are not to know them; when you will be present, but yet must be absent. I shall leave the explanation and application of these . paradoxes to your own good sense, which, I have no doubt, will soon satisfy you as to the meaning of them. Were I required to pourtray a good domestic servant, I should say, *he* must have *eyes* like a *hawk,* but be as *blind* as a *bat; ears* like a *cat,* but be as *deaf* as a *post;* must have more *sensibility* than the *sensitive plant,* but yet be as *hard* as a *stone;* be *wise* as a *counsellor,* yet *ignorant* as an *ass;* his *movement swift* as that of an *eagle,* but *smooth* as that of a *swallow;* in *manners* and *politeness* a *Frenchman,* in *probity* and *virtue* an *Englishman;* in dress a *gentleman;* in *disposition a saint; in activity a harlequin; in gravity a judge:* he must have a *lady's hand,* a *maiden speech,* and a *light foot;* in *protection* and *defence* a *lion;* in confidence and trust like the law of the *Medes* and *Persians,* " which altereth not ; " in domestic management a *Moses;* in *chastity* a *Joseph;* in *pious resolution* a *Joshua;* in *wisdom* a *serpent;* in *innocence* a *dove.* I shall leave these remarks to your serious consideration, and hoping the good hand of the Lord will be with you to direct your steps aright, I shall conclude with the Apostle PAUL's admonition, when he desires his son Titus to " *exhort servants to be obedient to their own masters, not answering again; not purloining, but showing all good fidelity; that they may adorn the doctrine of God our Saviour in all things.*"—Titus, chap. ii. ver. 9, 10. " *Not with eye-service, as menpleasers; but as the servants of Christ, doing the will of God from the heart; with good will doing service as to the Lord, and not to men: knowing that whatsoever good thing any man doeth, the same shall he receive of the Lord, whether he is* BOND *or* FREE." And to masters also he saith, " *And, ye masters, do the same things unto them, forbearing threatening, knowing that your Master also is in heaven; neither is there respect of persons with him.*"—Ephesians, chap. vi. ver. 5, 9.

TO BUTLERS.

I SHALL now, William, make a few observations to you on butlers; as you have already got promoted in your situation, and I have no doubt, with a continuance of good behaviour, and study how to do your work well, that you will soon be able to take a butler's place; and the directions which I shall give to you will suit Edward, and James, and others under the same circumstances, if ever they should get promoted, or offer themselves for that situation.

I am well aware, William, that I am now treading on tender ground with many who are butlers, or rather fill up the place of butlers, from whom I expect no thanks for the observations which I shall make respecting them; but it is for your sake, and for a few more who are not above learning, that I offer my remarks. You are well aware, that in several families, where you have been acquainted with the servants, constant confusion has taken place through the persons who have been in the butler's situation not knowing their business properly. It is a great trouble to ladies and gentlemen when they are so unfortunate as to be imposed on in this manner, and very disagreeable to the rest of the servants. But I shall proceed to notice a few things which are necessary for you, or any one else who wishes for a butler's situation, to know.

In the first place, it is indispensably necessary that you thoroughly understand the art of properly waiting at table and conducting a dinner-party; indeed, you ought to know how every thing should be done, in point of waiting, whether at dinner, supper, or breakfast: and whether you have nerves sufficient to carry you through it. There are numbers of servants who know well how to wait at table when there is a peron at the head who can arrange and take the trust and command of the dinner; but if it so happens that they have the directing of others, they often cause great confusion and mistakes; this some cannot help, through being nervous, and others through being careless in not observing when they have seen a dinner-party conducted well; therefore, neither of those two characters ought to attempt to take a butler's place. There are many good and useful servants who are only fit to *be led*, but not *to lead* others, and if it happens that they are moved out of their accustomed sphere, it only makes them uncomfortable, and often causes sad confusion in a family. It is not only necessary that you should know your business and have sufficient nerves to manage a dinner-party, &c. &c. but that you should know how to conduct yourself on such occasions, and indeed on all others, as, when you are butler, you will have persons to do the chief of the work, but it will rest with you to see that all is done properly; therefore, you will always have a care on your mind, or at least ought to have, that every thing should be done in an orderly manner, and at a proper time.

The butler in respectable families has the looking after the whole of the men-servants; and, where there is not a housekeeper, most of the women-servants are under his cognizance, as far as their honesty and good behaviour are concerned. In many families the ladies and gentlemen give their orders to the butler to be delivered to the other servants; in such cases, always carry them in a respectful way, not in a domineering manner, for this shows ignorance and ill-breeding as well as a weak mind. Deliver your orders and messages likewise as coming from your master and mistress, so as not to make too much use of the pronoun *I*. It will be your place to see that the rest of the servants have proper and necessary things, and keep them for the use which they are intended for; and likewise that each servant does the work which he may have undertaken to do, as there often occurs much confusion from some of the servants not doing their work in an orderly way, and in its proper time. If you should find some obstinate and impertinent to you, reason with them on the impropriety of such conduct, and how it will hurt their character if you name it to their master or mistress. If at any time you should find it necessary to admonish or correct any of your fellow-servants, let it be done in an humble spirit, that they may see you have their

good and welfare at heart; never try to provoke or
irritate their feelings on purpose to make them say
or do things, that you may have some plausible excuse to insult or injure them; this many butlers do
to gain their wicked ends, that they may have
something to run to their master or mistress with,
that their eyes and ears may be shut against the
rest of the servants, if they should happen to speak
of the bad conduct of the butler; therefore, be
you on your guard to do the thing which is right
and just. You will at times find it necessary to
exert all the power you have placed in you by your
master or mistress, as some servants are so unruly
and insulting, unless they are kept in their proper
places, that there will be no peace in the family: to
such persons as those be firm in your demands and
just in your principles; if they should be hasty or
passionate, or any way affected with liquor when
you speak to them, and they behave saucily and in-
solently to you, do not say much to them while in
such a state, wait till another opportunity, and
then reason with them; tell them the evil consequences of such behaviour, and that if there is
not an acknowledgment made, you must acquaint
your master or mistress: by doing this you will
give them time to reflect and repent; if they do
so, let it not go further, but *forgive* the insult
freely; let them see that you know how to rule
and forgive; and never run up to a master or mistress with complaints of your fellow-servants if you

can anywise avoid it, for two reasons: first, it must be very unpleasant to ladies and gentlemen to have their servants quarrelling and bringing complaints against each other, and perhaps giving notice to leave all in a hurry, when the master or mistress knows not for what or for why. Whenever you see your fellow-servants quarrelling with each other, use your authority to separate them and to admonish the aggressor, and try to settle the matter amicably; be careful not to judge partially, endeavour to set things in a clear light between them, admonish error, and establish right; and try all in your power to keep your fellow-servants in peace with each other: by doing this you will gain their respect and love, and you will find it a pleasure to rule in a family where you are respected by your fellow-servants and have the confidence of your employers. In the second place, if you be hasty in running to a master or mistress with complaints of your fellow-servants, consider what injury you may do them, as a stain on their character may be the ruin of them for ever; but if you are obliged to do so, be careful that you do not heighten the fault by a gross representation of it, which is wicked and cruel. Consider that servants' characters are their bread and their all, therefore to injure them unjustly in this respect is as great a crime as if you robbed them of every thing that they had in the world.

If you should have a brother, or sister, or any

other relation, in the same family you live with, do not judge partially if any thing occurs between them and the other servants, as much discontent is caused when this is the case. Consider, when you are at the head of a family, it is your place to see that each servant does his or her work properly, and all behave as they ought to do; you are then as it were a master, or judge, and must know no person to show them partiality, not even to a brother, sister, nor even to a wife, if she was living with you and had done wrong; but rather be more severe to them than to the others, that your fellow-servants may see that you act with uprightness, which will make them the more obedient to you.

You must remember that the eyes of the servants are always open to see the faults and partiality of the upper servants, and it is too often the case that the bare names of a butler and housekeeper are sufficient for some servants to abuse and speak against them; be careful you never give them a just cause to do so, but be an example in all things which are honest and praiseworthy. Let them see by your assiduity and attention to your master and mistress, that you have their comfort at heart. Remember, the most ignorant servant can see things which are not right and just in another, therefore be not merely an eye-servant, but do the same in their presence as behind their back: for it is too often the case that upper servants will do nothing unless it is in the presence of their employers, or where they can be noticed; those persons are what the Scripture calls *eye-servants*.

Whenever you are so unfortunate as to do wrong, never attempt to justify it to your fellow-servants, for how can you expect them to respect and cheerfully obey you if you do? Consider well when a person is in authority, and does not the thing which is right, what a burden the rest of the servants have upon them. Suppose a person in authority gets drunk, steals, or is neglectful in business, how can he, when he sees others guilty of the same thing, admonish them for so doing? he has, by his own act, put all power from himself, for the answer is ready in a moment, *You did the same; if you tell of me, I will of you;* therefore confusion is the consequence, and the master and mistress suffer through it. When the butler's mouth is stopped, his eyes must be blinded, and his hands, which should protect his master's property, are paralyzed; therefore be watchful over your own conduct; keep yourself at a proper distance from the servants under you; do not be too familiar with them, but be affable and ready to do any thing for them at a moment of need; there will be times when you must be affable one among the other, at merry-makings, on particular occasions; only observe, never to be off your guard, nor suffer any unbecoming behaviour among your fellow-servants: if you are to be merry, *be wise* also. Never allow any licentious conversation, it is wicked ; nor suffer the men-servants to be twisting and turning the words of the females to some filthy meaning, as is too often done in gentlemen's service. I have been at places where the females have been afraid to open their mouths to speak before the men-servants, on account of their putting some obscene and offensive meaning to every word they have spoken; this is true blackguardism, which never ought to be suffered in a gentleman's house. You must be aware that you will have various tempers to deal with; make it your study how to govern and direct the family affairs with honour and credit to yourself, the comfort of your employers, and the welfare of your fellow-servants. Never attempt to take a place which you are not competent to manage; many servants do this; then, to make up their deficiency in ability, they turn tale-bearers to their employers, so that they stop in the family a little while, then get turned out like what they are; but I hope, my young friends, you will act otherwise, and recommend yourselves by *well-doing*, the best and happiest means which you can adopt.

SHUTTING UP THE HOUSE, &c.

I SHALL now address myself to you, Joseph and Edward, concerning the fastening and shutting up the house and the gate of the area at night, as it in general belongs to the man-servant to do it, or to see that it is done. A mistake here may be of fatal consequence to yourself as well as to those whom you serve, therefore it behoves you to pay particular attention to it. In the first place, when you go to shut up the parlour or drawing-room shutters, let your hands be clean, that you may not dirty the paint; see that the sashes are made fast before you put the shutters to; when this is done, then close the shutters and see that they are properly fastened. If there are bells to the shutters and doors, let them be put up, or, if the shutters and doors be secured by an *alarm-bell*, be sure to put the wire of the alarm-bell to them, so that they cannot be opened without its going off. Let those rooms which are not used be shut up as soon as the dusk of the evening comes on, for at this time many houses have been robbed, particularly by the kitchen and lower parts of the house, through the area-gate being left unlocked; therefore be careful to have it locked before dusk. Be particular in fastening up the street-door the last thing; let the chain be up and the bolts sent quite home; indeed, take every precaution to prevent thieves from getting into the house. If you live with single ladies you must be doubly diligent in fastening up the house, for two reasons; first, that thieves are more likely to attempt to break in; and, secondly, you will have no gentleman to overlook you to see that you have fastened the places up safe; therefore consider, if the house should be robbed through your neglect, it will be of very serious consequence to your character; and be always on your guard to have every place fastened up in proper time, as this is what neither of you have had to do as yet, and of course you are the more likely to forget it. If you are not tall enough to reach to put the shutters to, have some short steps, or a stool, which in general is kept for that purpose, for you ought never to get the drawing-room and parlour chairs to stand on, as is too often done.

CONFIDENCE AND HONESTY.

In keeping accounts, your confidence and honesty will be put to the test, as it will be a trial of your integrity, both as to yourself and those whom you may have the honour to serve. To wrong yourself, through paying for things and not putting them down, is bad; but to put down more than what you have laid out for the family, is worse; for in one you pay for your neglect and inattention to yourself, while, in the other, you sin against God, bring yourself under the strong arm of the law, trouble your conscience, break the confidence which has been placed in you, and overwhelm yourself with a host of difficulties and disgrace.

To avoid this, have an account-book to put down every thing you pay for, both for the family and yourself; let the money which you expend in the course of the day be put down as you lay it out, or every night before you go to bed, as you never ought to lie down to sleep till this is done; for if you trust to your memory day after day, it will be no wonder if you make mistakes, as you will forget what you have paid for, and very likely the price of some things which you do know: in so doing you will be at a loss yourself, or must put down more, or things which you never have bought, to make up the deficiency. If you do the latter, and the family find it out, it will be but a poor excuse to say, that you have laid out so much, and that you are so much short, therefore you only did it to make up the difference, not to cheat them. Although this may be true, and you may not have the least desire to wrong or cheat, still how can your master or mistress know this, as any person who does ever so much wrong in cheating their employers may say the same? Therefore if at any time you lose your money, through forgetting to put down the things you have spent it in, tell your employers that you have forgot something which you have bought for the family, rather than as before mentioned; and if they make it up to you, be careful that you do not forget it again; or if they do not make it up to you, let it increase in you a spirit of diligence to keep a more correct and proper account for your own sake; therefore have one book for your general use, to put down every thing which you lay out for the family yourself, or any body else, and another in which you can put down from this general book all which you have laid out for the family.

In most families they pay their servants once a week; but if you have time, cast up every night what you have laid out during the day, and likewise the money you have in your pocket: by doing this, if you should have forgotten any thing, it may bring it to your mind; or, if you cannot cast it up every night, do it once or twice every week; this will be to the benefit of your pocket and the ease of your mind, for it is very perplexing to be constantly losing small sums of money week after week, and our employers certainly neither want our money nor wish for it: but I would rather have you forget and be the loser by your bad memory, than give your mind to a dishonest and thievish way of putting down things which have never been had, or adding a few pence to those which you have been instructed to buy; for the consequence will be, that our employers will reason thus: "If my servant would rob me of a few pence, he would of shillings; and if of shillings, he would of pounds, if in his power to do it." For it is manifest that it is the same dishonest principle which tempts one to take a few pence, that tempts another to take thousands of pounds; and the only difference is, that he who has taken the thousands of pounds has had a greater opportunity of satisfying his thievish appetite, than the other who took the few pence; but the principle of both is the same, therefore a highwayman is a more honourable person than a dishonest servant, as the highwayman breaks no confidence, for no person puts any in him. He may likewise have the excuse of the most urgent want, while a servant has no particular distress to drive him to practise such abominable evil. The highwayman may rob to satisfy the wants of nature, while the servant is trying to satisfy a corrupt mind, which never can or will be satisfied, even if it had a thousand times as much as those he serves. Therefore to give way to a discontented and covetous temper, is the sure way to lead to disgrace, trouble, and affliction, and often ends in ignominy and death. How many, my young friends, have I seen come to this, whose prospects would have been bright and cheering to themselves and friends, had they continued in the honest and humble path which the good hand of Providence placed them in; but by giving way to a covetous disposition they have blasted all their prospects, comforts, and character, and turned out like vagabonds, a disgrace to themselves and a dishonour to their relations and friends.

I shall now offer to you, my young friends, a few reflections for your consideration on this important point, and I wish you well to consider them, particularly before you attempt to commit so great an evil as theft and breaking your confidence. Suppose that you could cheat your employers of a few pence, nay, a few shillings or pounds, without being found out: now answer the following questions: Is this the way you would wish your servants, if you kept any, to act towards you? Is there no conscience to torment and tell you you have done wrong? And suppose every person should do the same thing one to another, what peace or confidence would there be in society if this was universally acted up to? or are you sure that there is no life after death, wherein those who have worked righteousness and acted justly will be rewarded? And are you sure, that those who have done wickedly, and broken every confidence that was put in them, shall not be punished? Have you no fear lest you should be found out? Do you not often tremble when you hear persons talking, that such and such a person was detected in dishonest ways? would you not fear that something would lead to a discovery of your wicked conduct, or that you may be found out, and disgraced before your fellow-servants and in the eyes of the world? Is there nothing in all this to put a damp on your spirit when tempted to act in a dishonest way? Think it over in your mind, and reflect that there must be something in these questions that will deter you from doing or acting dishonestly. Consider, what will a few shillings or a few pounds avail you, or any other servant, if he loses his character? For, if you rob your employers, how can you expect a character? And if they should keep you afterwards, they never can respect or put any confidence in you, as they may have done before. Your fellow-servants, too, must look upon you with disdain and contempt, as bringing a dishonour on their profession; they cannot respect you as they have done before. Your friends will be ashamed of you in bringing a disgrace upon them, and perhaps would never look upon you again, while you may be discharged without a character and be obliged to go about like a vagabond, if you escape being *transported* or *hanged*. I have seen many instances of this kind in the course of my service, and some in persons after living in families a number of years, and having had many favours shown to them, and being promoted and respected by their employers, and who might have moved in the sphere of life in which it had pleased God to put them, all the days of their life, with honour and comfort to themselves, if they had not given way to a dishonest and covetous principle. I have known many servants, after having lived a number of years in families, keep back the money which they had received to pay the tradesmen's bills with; and not only this, but actually forge or sign their names to the bills, by doing which they have committed a *felony*, and might have been hanged for it, if the families had prosecuted them. Consider what must be the feelings of persons who have been respected in the sphere of life in which they have moved, and have had almost every comfort and blessing of society, and perhaps lived to the age of thirty, forty, or fifty years with respect and credit to themselves and to the honour of those whom they served; but, alas! have given way to a dishonest disposition, which has at last thrown them on the world, despised and scouted, under the displeasure of a benevolent master and mistress, and obliged to forego all future acquaintance with kind and agreeable fellow-servants; instead of which they are tormented by their own upbraiding conscience always at hand, saying, "All those troubles you have brought on yourself through your own misconduct." Consider well, my young friends, that our time here is but short; our wants will not be long, and we cannot take any thing away with us; if we keep this reflection in our minds, and recollect also the uncertainty of life, this will in some measure abate our anxiety to get money. I have known many to be over-anxious to amass a certain sum, and when gained they have not lived to enjoy it; others have been wishing to add a little more to what they had, thinking that then they should be happy.

But, alas! they have got it, but no happiness has come with it; while others desiring to get rich all in a hurry, have launched out in an unsafe way, and have even lost that which they had already acquired; such is the uncertainty of things pertaining to this life. I therefore hope that each of you will consider the foregoing observations, and I am sure you will find honesty is the best policy; and a good character and approving conscience, truer sources of happiness than any that worldly greatness or riches can give.

MARKETING, PAYING BILLS, &c.

It perhaps may come within your office to go to market, and in some families the man-servant has to pay the bills to the tradesmen; it will therefore be necessary for you to take notice of the good or bad quality of different articles; likewise to get acquainted with the real value of them. In going to market always seek for the best things, unless ordered to the contrary; but then you must take care that you are not charged an exorbitant price for them, pay the fair value and no more. If a tradesman can afford to give you a shilling when you lay out a few pounds with him, accept it, but never ask for it, nor even accept it if you have the least idea that he has overcharged for the goods, in order to give it you;

always keep clear of this, or you cannot be at full liberty to speak if you see any thing wrong. If at any time you should discover that a tradesman is cheating your master, tell him of it; if he acknowledge his fault and rectify it, take no more notice of it, but look carefully after him for the future. Never desire to change an old tradesman. One who has perhaps served the family many years may do a thing which may not be quite right; in duty to your employers, you ought to tell him of it, but in charity to him let it go no farther, if he make good what is wrong. Many servants being dishonest themselves, will, when they first go to a place, endeavour to get all the old tradespeople changed, that they may be enabled to carry on their theft and wickedness without being discovered: this conduct is as cruel as it is dishonest. Never buy things for the family, of persons who bring them to the door, or hawk them about the streets, unless you are a very good judge of the nature of them, as they are generally in such cases of an inferior quality. If, however, you should be induced to do it, never compare the article so bought in point of price with one of the same kind bought at a regular tradesman's. This is both dishonourable and unjust. Recollect the tradesman keeps his shop open all the year, through various seasons, and takes the chance of various market prices himself. He likewise has to pay generally a heavy rent and taxes, wages, and poor rates, all which expenses those wandering hawkers are without; added to which, you always expect the trades-man's goods to be what they really appear and what you ask for; therefore, on every account you ought not to tempt a master or mistress into making any comparison to the disadvantage of those they may be in the habit of employing. When you pay bills have them properly signed, and be particular in taking the change, &c.; have a book to enter your accounts in, and make every tradesman sign his name in it as well as to the bills; you will find it handy to refer to at any time, as there are often mis-takes by bills being sent in twice over.

ANSWERING THE BELLS, AND OPENING THE DOOR, &c. &c.

WHENEVER you hear the drawing-room or par-lour bells ring, go up immediately to see what is wanted, unless you know what it is for. If you cannot go that very moment, do it as soon as you possibly can, and if you should be dress-ing, &c. so that you cannot go for some minutes, arrange it with one of your fellow-servants to go for you. When you have to take a candle with you, mind that you carry it upright, so as not to drop the grease on the stairs; and never take it into the room where the company is, but set it down at the outside of the door; be careful that the bottom of it is not greasy.

When you go in and out of the rooms, let it be done without making a noise in opening or shutting the doors. Sometimes when the wind blows, and one of the windows is open, you can scarcely avoid slamming the door, unless you keep the handle firm in your hand till you have shut it. Be as quick as possible in answering the rings of the front door, as you must suppose it cannot be pleasant, or proper, for any body to be kept waiting. A little time is of great consequence to some persons, and particularly to tradespeople who may have another appointment to attend to; consider also that whenever you delay unnecessarily going to the door, or answering the bells, you are off your duty and culpable for being so.

When you hear a double knock at the street-door, before you go to open it you should inquire if the family will be at home to see company, and if not to all, learn to whom they will, so that you make no confusion when you are asked the question. When you open the street-door to double knocks, always throw it wide open, but not so as to drive the key or the handle through the wall, which some have done, to the great disfiguring of it, but which will be avoided by holding the handle firm in your hand, by which means you will be able to stop the door the moment you please. When you stand with it open, advance toward the sill of the door to receive or answer any message. If you let

the company in, show them into the room to the
family, or the room which is appointed to see
company in; set chairs for the company round the
fire if in winter; if not, put them near the place
where the family sit; and if they should not be in
the room, let them know immediately. If the company are seen in the parlour, you need not stop to
shut the street-door, if more than one person
comes in, but deliver the names, and then go
back and shut the door; at night, however, you
must not do so, but let the company come into the
hall, then shut the door; if you live where there are
two men-servants kept, let one open the door, and
the other announce the names, and set the chairs,
&c.

When your master or mistress rings for you to
let the visitors out, open the street-door wide, and do
not shut it till they have withdrawn from before the
door, whether they have a carriage or not; for, to
shut the door whilst they are still in the front of it, is
disrespectful and a breach of good manners.

If there should be a double knock at night, and
your family do not expect company, you must not
in this case open the door wide, but put the chain
up, which is for this purpose, and will let the door
open wide enough until you know who knocks;
but if you expect company, let the door, whether
by day or by night, be opened as *wide* as it *can*, to
let them in, as it is very rude only to open it a little

when you answer double knocks.   Be particular in
giving in the names of the company; let it be done
in an audible voice, and properly pronouncing the
name of each person ; if you do not rightly understand it, ask a second time rather than make a blun-
der in giving in a wrong one.

Always have a slate with a pencil, or some paper
with pens and ink, in the hall, or near at hand, in
case any lady or gentleman should come when your
family is not at home, and want to write; if this were
kept in all the halls, there would not be so many
houses robbed as there are ; but never suffer any
lady or gentleman (who may come with a double
knock), if you do not know them, to be left alone, or
to go into any of the rooms under any pretence
whatever, unless you stop the whole time with
them.

There is another thing you must be on your
guard against, particularly if you live with single
ladies, or with married ones when the gentleman is
not at home.   There will be persons come with a
double knock, and ask for the ladies with all the assurance imaginable, pretending to know the whole
of the family. If it is a person you do not know, and
your lady is at home, you can do no less than show
him into the room where she sees her company : if
she is in the room when you announce his name,
you can judge whether she knows him or not, by
her manner of receiving him ; if you cannot, wait
at the outside of the door till you hear whether

they begin to converse together as if they were acquainted; if they do, of course you will go away directly; but if not, wait at the door till the stranger departs. You can let your lady know that you are near the door by coughing, if she has not given you directions how to act on such occasions. Many ladies have been robbed and ill-treated by persons of this description, therefore be on your guard, and particularly if the lady's relations are abroad, or officers, as such are more apt to be imposed on than others; for persons will learn the particulars of the family, and knowing that some of them are abroad, can contrive to get an interview with the lady, under the pretence that they are just come from them, or something of that kind; therefore never be out of call at such times.

NOT AT HOME.

I SHALL now, James, make a few observations to you concerning saying " *Not at home*," when in reality the family are at home; as I consider your conduct in refusing to say " Not at home," when your master or mistres gives you orders to do so, unjustifiable for two or three reasons, which I shall point out to you. I am much pleased with your tenderness of conscience in not wishing to tell a falsehood, and God forbid that you should think me careless of the truth, because I wish to prove to you in what sense you tell no falsehood in saying your employers are *not at home* when they really are at home. I therefore wish you and all my young friends to pay particular attention while I am speaking to you on this point. In all states and kingdoms they have their peculiar ways, and manner of secrecy, in carrying on the system of moral and political government, which it would not become the under agents, who might be employed to assist in any executive part thereof, to *tell* or *divulge* to any person who may think proper to ask them things which they are intrusted with the knowledge of. In every state, trade, and family, there are secrets which the inmates ought not to divulge, for, if they did, it would be a breach of their duty to those whom they serve: for instance, if you go into a shop to purchase an article, and you think proper to ask the shopman what it cost his master at first hand, do you think it would be his duty to tell you? surely not. Neither would it be proper to give an impertinent answer to the person who asks the question, for fear he should lose his master a customer. The shopman's business is not to know what his master gives for articles, but what he sells them for ; this is what he is engaged to do : if he tells the other to any person who may think proper to ask him, he is not doing his duty ; and no one would employ such a person in his shop if he knew he did so. What confidence could there be between man and man, if we were all obliged to satisfy every person who asked us respecting any point he wished to know? I understand no persons are suffered to live in the Royal Family, that is, in the King's household, without first taking an oath *that they will know nothing but their own business,* that is, not divulge any thing they see and hear that belongs to His Majesty and his family. This is what ought to be; for, how distressing would be the thought to any family, and particularly to one of such exalted rank, if the domestic servants were obliged to tell the secrets of the family they live with to any inquisitive person who may think fit to question them, merely because they deem it telling a lie to say " I don't know." This would surely be carrying things too far; for, if it were acted up to, a family would be afraid to take a servant into their house. I have sometimes gone to a tradesman's for a thing which I have wanted, and he has said that he had not any of it, when at the same time I knew he had, but he would not admit he told a lie, neither did I consider him as doing so; for, when he said he had none, he meant *not any* to *sell* or *dispose* of to a purchaser, as he had it only for his own use, and not to be sold. I hope, James, this reasoning may remove any thing of an unpleasant feeling on the subject from your mind. Let me hear, therefore, what you have to say.

James. I cannot but say, Sir, that you have put the question concerning saying " *Not at home* " in a fresh light; but still my doubts are not all removed

2

as to the correctness of this representation, as I
think the holy Scriptures are against it; particularly as some servants have said, that, as their
masters and mistresses have taught them to tell lies
for them, there can be no harm in telling a few,
when convenient, for themselves. It is a sad thing
to sanction any thing against the Word of God;
and, if a disregard to truth were followed up in
every respect, it would destroy the confidence and
peace of the community at large, as much as the
divulging of secrets could do. In the Epistle to
Titus, the Apostle Paul exhorts us to use " *sound
speech, that cannot be condemned;*" and St. John,
in the Revelations, xxii. 15, tells us, that " *who-
soever loveth and maketh a lie shall not enter
heaven.*"

Onesimus. Far be it from me, James, to make
you think less of that blessed book which has been
given us to enlighten our dark understandings,
and point out the path of duty towards God and
our neighbour, and in what our true happiness
consists. I hope I shall evermore be thankful for
so great a mercy as this is, and show, by a humble
walk and conversation before God and man, that I
revere the book and reverence the divine Author of
it: but observe, the Apostle is exhorting his son
Titus to use plainness and soundness in speech on
the doctrines of the Gospel, which some who had
set themselves up as teachers did not do; and, not
only this, but it was then, as it is now, customary

to use ambiguous expressions, on purpose to defraud and deceive persons, therefore the Apostle
exhorts Titus to do the contrary. And as to St.
John, you must notice what he saith; " HE THAT
LOVETH" is the person pointed out: if you do it,
it is not because you love it, or because you make
a profit by it; thousands utter falsehoods to defraud
each other; and others to kill time, as they say, in
telling what they are pleased to call innocent lies,
in romancing and talking to amuse themselves. It
is for such conduct as this that God will bring them
into judgment. Now, admitting that saying " *Not
at home*," when people really are at home, is a *lie*,
it cannot be so in the same sense as the others; but
ladies and gentlemen do not think it is telling lies
when they order their servants to say " *Not at
home*;" they consider it only as a mere form, and
that they are not at home to see visitors; not but I
could wish that some other form should be made
use of, in order that the ignorant might have no
stumbling-stone laid in their path. But remember,
that if you should be called into a court of justice,
there is nothing upon earth, not a master or mistress, no not even a father or any other relation
whatever, must hinder you from speaking the *naked
truth*, let it be on what subject it may. If you
know what you are called upon to say, utter what
you know, neither more nor less.

James. I am very glad to ease my mind by
viewing the subject in the broad sense in which you

place it; but the worst of it is, that granting it is not telling a lie merely to say " Not at home," when we know the meaning of the expression is taken as is intended, yet this way of speaking, innocent as it may be in itself, often leads us into a long string of false assertions, extremely painful for those to make use of, who at all other times accustom themselves to the strictest truth. But there are some persons who will take no denial, and will ask, " How long have they been gone out? Which way did they go?" and at last, when I have taken up the name to my mistress, she will make me run after the very persons who have just had positive denials, and bring them back again, which seems worse than all.

Onesimus. I certainly do not approve of ladies and gentlemen asking so many particulars; but be as sharp in your answers as you possibly can consistently with proper respect: and as to running after the persons to call them back, if the lady or gentleman should want to see them, this I think nothing of, as you can easily say, " My master, or mistress, will be at home to you, Sir, or Ma'am." They will understand it: therefore always take a name up directly.

You will also often have to answer the door to a number of persons who come with begging PETITIONS: many make a trade of going with them from one place to another; and through this, and the frequent impositions that are practised on gen-

tlepeople, they will very seldom see any. There
are, however, a number of ladies and gentlemen
who would relieve a poor distressed creature if they
knew they were real objects of charity ; if, therefore, you live with a charitable family, and you
can possibly look into the case yourself, before you
take up the petition to your master or mistress, you
may be enabled to speak as to the truth of it ; as
there is no way wherein the poor can approach the
rich unless it be by petition, for in the street they
will not look at or listen to them. In doing as I
advise, and visiting the chambers of the distressed,
you will learn to be humble and thankful for your
own situation and the blessings you enjoy above the
unfortunate persons whom you have been to see.
If their distress should be through their carelessness and inattention, or wicked living, or any kind
of misconduct, let it admonish you to be careful not
to do the same things, seeing the ill effects of a bad
life. You will also have an opportunity of assisting a little yourself, if ever so little; for, " BLESSED
is HE who considereth the poor to relieve them, for
the end of that man will be peace;" and you will
enjoy more comfort in this life by giving a little to
ease the necessities of the poor, than in spending
ten times as much in pleasurable sin, which can
never satisfy or bring any true comfort of mind.

ON GOING OUT VISITING, &c. &c.

In walking out with the ladies, you must keep near enough to them, for people to see that you are their servant, lest they should be insulted by some of the monsters in human shape, that cannot let a modest woman go along the street without trying to put her to the blush. Be particularly on your guard when you walk out with young ladies, as sometimes they, being inexperienced, will turn back to look at those fops and impertinent men who cannot let a lady pass them without staring her out of countenance; and who sometimes will have the impertinence to ask the servant who the ladies are. If ever this happens to you, reply civilly, that your duty forbids you to mention their names to any person in the street. No gentleman can blame you for such a reply as this.

Be particular in your dress when you walk out, and have gloves on; most families allow them for this purpose. When gentlemen's servants are walking out with the ladies, they themselves are often insulted by a set of ignorant wretches, who will at other times lick the dust of their shoes if they will give them a good *tuck-out*, as they call it, if they should happen to come to the house on any business; and, as soon as they have had what they wanted, they will turn and abuse the giver. When. ever you are insulted by such vulgar people, treat them with silent contempt, as it will not do for you to get into a quarrel with them; but if any body insults the ladies, defend them with all your strength and might, as the law will protect you from any serious consequences, as you are only doing your duty. If you should be walking out with the ladies when a gentleman is with them, and they talk in an under voice, so that you may not hear, you can easily keep at a greater distance than when there is no gentleman with them. If you have to walk after the ladies in the night at any time, as sometimes, when they are out in fine weather, they will walk home, you must keep nearer to them than if it was day, or else they will get insulted by some blackguard fellow or other; but if there is a gentleman with them, you will not be required to be so near.

In crossing the street you must be very careful, for an accident may happen in a moment, as there are so many things to take the attention in town, and carriages travel at so rapid a rate. Some ladies are so thoughtless in not looking about them, that a fatal accident may happen in a moment; therefore, if the ladies are off their guard, be not you off *your duty*; look out for them, and, if danger is near, warn them of it in time. If you know the house you are going to, advance, when you are within twenty yards of it, before your ladies, and give a double knock, as some servants are a long time before they answer the door; they will then not be kept waiting. If the ladies go a-shopping, when you see them intending to go into one, and the door should be shut, step forward and open it for them, and then shut it again. In knocking at a gentleman's door you should not ring the bell, unless you see it written on a brass plate to do so, except it should be at a relation's of the family which you live with, then you always should ring as well as knock, and also at your own door, as this is a mark of respect, and a hint to the family and the servants that some of the family are come home. Knock loud enough to be heard, as some of the halls and kitchens are a great way from the front door. When the servant comes to the door, ask if the family be at home; ask for them by name, for fear of a mistake. If at home, give the names of those whom you are with. Do it with an AUDIBLE *voice* and a *distinct pronunciation*, that the other servant may not be at a loss to give in the name. If they are not at home, you will have to give a card to the servant; and as in general the footmen have to carry the cards, you should have a little case to put them in, to keep them clean. If the family are admitted, and you have to wait in the hall, keep yourself quiet, and do not deface the wall or floor of the hall with your cane or umbrella. I have seen some persons amuse themselves at such times by writing their names, or making letters or figures, on the wall or floor, which is highly foolish and improper. Neither do it yourself, nor suffer it to be done where you live by another. Whenever you go out, either with the carriage, or to walk, be sure to have visiting cards and money with you, as you will perhaps have to pay for something.

If you have to go out with a carriage, as soon as it comes to the door put the blinds down, and the farther glass up; but if it rains, do not put the blinds down till the family are just going to get in; when you put down the glasses, or put up the blinds of the carriage, do not get into it with your dirty shoes, as the coachmen have enough to do without cleaning after you; if you cannot do it without, let down the steps and kneel on the edge of the sill of the carriage where the door shuts; if the carriage be one which opens, you must be very careful that you do not attempt to do it when the glasses are up, for, if you do, you will most likely break them, which will be of serious consequence, as they are very expensive. When you receive directions where you are to go to, if your family are in the carriage, turn your head sideways, and do not put your mouth just into their faces while they are speaking, as you cannot hear with your mouth; and besides, you may in that case breathe into theirs, rather more than may be agreeable. When you have got your directions where to go, get up behind the carriage before you attempt to tell the coachman; give the number of the house first, and the square, street, or place next: but be very particular both in receiving and giving them, as you will find it sometimes almost impossible to hear for the noise of the passing carriages. Be careful in getting up and down, as an accident may soon happen. I know a man who was well and hearty, and met with an accident from behind the carriage which obliged him to have his leg cut off: he told me there were not three hours between his setting out from home and his leg being taken off. If you lean forward a little on your toes, you will ride much easier; but do not scratch the hind pannel of the carriage with your nails, or the top with your umbrella, as idle silly boys will do; and be careful not to scratch the front pannels of the carriage in opening or shutting the door, or with the umbrella, in holding it over the ladies while getting in, as the points of the umbrella will scratch it in a moment if you are not careful. In going through turnpike gates you must observe if the man who receives the tolls be on the right side of you, to hold fast with the holders on the left side with your left hand; or if the tollman should be on the left side, then hold fast with the right hand, of the holders on the right; this will prevent any accident occurring through the coachman's going off before you can get yourself upright. If you take hold of the left-hand holder with your right hand, and lean over the left side of the carriage to pay the toll-man, and the coachman should move on before you have recovered yourself, the consequence may be fatal to you, as you will be pulled between the wheel and the body of the carriage, and have no power to save yourself. There is likewise a trick of the tollmen, which is not a very pleasant one: when it is a dirty, or dark night, they will let the money slip through their hands, and will not attempt to pick it up, but rather shuffle it in the mud with their feet, as they know you cannot stop to look after it ; I have been served thus several times; therefore, hold the money tight in your hand till they have put their hand into yours. When you have your orders to go to any gentleman's house, and only have the street and the number of the house, knock at the door, then go to the carriage to know who you are to ask for; by doing this you will save time. Be particular in preventing the ladies' dress being dirtied by the wheels in getting in and out of the carriage. When the family have done with the carriage, put down the glasses and draw up the blinds ; and always when it rains, if the ladies get out for only a few minutes, pull the blinds up to keep the wet out. There is one thing I could wish you to be very particular about, as many fatal accidents have happened through the want of attention to it: it is, to turn the handle of the carriage door quite home, so as to let it have firm hold to keep it from flying open with the shaking of the carriage, which might endanger the pannel if any thing else should be coming by, at the time: but this is a trifling consideration compared

to the safety of children, who are too apt to lean
with their heads out of the windows, and if the door
should not be fast, the dreadful consequence may
be better imagined than I am willing to describe.
Consider what would be your feelings if such a
thing should happen from any carelessness of yours.
If the door will not hold fast, speak to your employers directly that you perceive it, and have it
altered : be careful, likewise, in opening and shutting it, that you do not pinch the children's fingers,
as they are not on their guard against such things,
and their poor little hands may be crushed in a
moment if you do not mind.

If at any time your employers should let you
sit with the coachman on the coach-box, which is
often done when the family take a little drive into
the country ; do not enter into licentious and filthy
conversation with him, as some servants have done,
which has caused them not to be permitted to
sit there any more. Do not laugh or talk loud
while you are on the box, as, when the carriage
windows are down, those within can hear every
thing you say, which must make it unpleasant to
them, and besides, it is disrespectful and improper
for a servant to do so ; therefore, whether you
are behind, or on the box, keep from laughing,
singing, or whistling, nor even talk any more
than what your business calls you to do. Always have an umbrella with you in the carriage,
as it will be handy to hold over the ladies in getting

in and out of the carriage, and likewise to preserve your own clothes from getting spoiled in case of sudden showers.

A servant who is acquainted with town, and well experienced in attending on persons at public places of amusement, is of great value to a family, and particularly to single ladies. Never order or tempt the coachman to break the ranks of the line that may be setting down at the place where you are going to: if the coachman is a regular one, this part of the business will rest with him. Be quick in opening the door, and see that the ladies' dresses do not touch the wheel. When an amusement is over, every one wants to get away as soon as possible; this causes great confusion, and serious accidents often occur through it; be particular therefore in asking those whom you attend, what time they will wish to come away. If you have a carriage, you must arrange with the coachman to be in good time to get near the door, that your family may be able to get in, and go away, without any difficulty. Consider well whether the place you choose is likely to be blocked up with other carriages; if so, it will not do to stand there, although it may be handy to get in, for that will be of no use unless you can also get away. When you have found a place for the carriage to stand, let the coachman keep there whilst you go to the door where you know the family will come out, and wait for them; but if they do not walk to the carriage, and will have it drive up to the door, the coachman must manage as well as he can, and not let himself get entangled in the midst of other carriages if he can any way help it. If you are with single ladies you must be doubly on your guard never to be behind your time, as they will be in a very awkward situation if you are not punctual; therefore, in that case, be rather before your time than after. You will find considerable difficulty at some private parties in getting up to the door, particularly if a great number be invited, and the street narrow. If the family prefer walking to the carriage, rather than wait to have it drawn up in a crowd, get it as near as you possibly can; and have ready their shawls, thick shoes, or whatever they may want: be in the hall, or near the door, to answer when called. If you are ordered to any particular time, and you are to let them know, be very exact in impressing it on the servants, as some are extremely negligent in not going up to let the families know when their servants are arrived. If you find they do not come, you had better ask the servants again if they have told your family; as in their bustle they may sometimes forget: but, if you are invariably punctual in attendance, perhaps your employers will look at their watch, and ask for you. Ladies and gentlemen who do so, are very strict in not ordering their carriage before they want it, and never keep their servants long waiting; while others will keep them by the hour standing in the cold and wet: but even then, my young friends, you must con sider, that when you are waiting for your family, you are only doing your duty; which you certainly are not doing when you keep the family waiting for you, but are guilty of a great breach of it, and which may be of much consequence at some particular times.

OF KNOWING TOWN.

So necessary is it for footmen to know town, and the residences of different families, that many ladies and gentlemen will not engage with any one who does not know town well, and has not been accustomed to go about visiting. They will give you the name of the person, and you must find the street and number yourself to direct the coachman : therefore, when you are in a place and do not know the visits, have a small book, such as you can put in your pocket; then, when you go to pay any visits with your family, or are sent to deliver cards, write down in it in alphabetical order the names of the persons you go to. This book you should always have with you, when you are out, as then, if you forget, you can easily refer to it. Whenever any ladies or gentlemen call at the place where you live, if they leave a card, write down the direction from it, if you do not know where they live; or if they are let in, you can ask the servant where they live : leave room under each letter to replace the name and residence when a change takes place; and appropriate one part of the book to setting down the different tradesmen, and their residence, as this will be of great service to you when you are sent out for any thing from them. Take notice, also, in the daytime, which end of the street the numbers begin at, so that if you go with the carriage at night, when dark, you may know where to find a house, without stopping the carriage to get down to look. I have known some footmen lose their place through not paying attention to this, as ladies and gentlemen cannot be always telling them, and some coachmen who live twenty years in a place are so stupid that they cannot get to know the round of visits, but depend entirely on the footman to direct them.

Boyle's " Court and Country Guide, and Town Visiting Directory," is kept in the hall by some families, on purpose to direct their servants where to find names and places of residence. It is a very useful book; but will often want fresh entries making, on account of those whom the family may visit changing their place of abode.

DELIVERING AND TAKING OUT CARDS.

LADIES are very particular in sending out cards when the family first comes to town, and receiving them in return. The footmen are intrusted with

the delivery of those cards, and if not done punc-
tually, it must of necessity cause confusion.   Families have even given up visiting each other on account of this form not being attended to.   Some
ladies give the servant a list of those whom he is to
take cards to ; if so, have a pencil with you, and as
you deliver them *mark* off each name delivered ;
this will prevent any mistake: keep the list by you,
or have a book to enter them into, and date them,
you can then refer to it at any time : indeed, if you
had a large book to enter what cards are taken
out, and what received, and likewise the dinner invi-
tations, and the evening parties, with the visits
paid and received, it would not only improve you
in writing, and teach you a little in the way of
book-keeping, but might perhaps amuse the
family for an hour, when in the country to see
whom they had visited when in town.   Always deliver your cards yourself, and take those which are
brought to the house to your master and mistress,
as soon as you have an opportunity.

TRAVELLING.

SOME servants have a great deal of travelling; and in
places where there is but one kept, there is a great
deal to do at such times to manage things well and
comfortably.   If there is a carriage to attend on,
and no coachman while travelling, it will fall to the
man servant to see it taken care of, particularly if

you live with a single lady. When the carriage is ordered to be ready to go out of town, see that it is greased and every part made secure and fit for travelling ; take a few nails, linch-pins, cords, and things of that kind, in case an accident should occur: some have them in a small box, which is fastened underneath the carriage. See to the trunks, covers, straps, and the apron of the carriage, the drag-chain, and the chain which goes behind the carriage to keep the trunk on. Be very particular in packing and loading the carriage, that nothing may be forgotten, and that the pannels of the carriage do not get scratched, as some of the stable-men are very careless. Make a memorandum of the parcels and things you take out at the inns that you stop at, on the road, and be very particular in not leaving them about, for there are dishonest servants as well as waiters, who are on the look-out at those places to take in persons who are not acquainted with life. Look to the wheels and other parts of the carriage every time before you set off, to see that all is right, and do not let your mistress be imposed on with bad horses, or in any other respect. While stopping at any place to change horses, if the family get out, keep your eye on the carriage, and if you have any refreshment, let it be in a room that will command a view of it, as there are persons at those places ready to run off with any thing if an opportunity offers itself. If the doors of the carriage will lock up, do it whenever you come to where the family get out ; also when you stop for the night. Always clean the inside of the carriage yourself, and see that those who clean the outside do not scratch it by using old dirty mops and leathers to do it with; as this is often the case. Make them likewise use plenty of water, or else, instead of washing the dirt off, they will rub it, and make the pannel look full of small scratches. If you go to a watering-place, or any where else to stop for any length of time, see to the carriage often, and have it kept under cover in the day, and locked up if you possibly can, that nothing may be lost out of it.

If you go to gentlemen's houses, there will be proper places for the carriage, and generally coachmen to take care of it; do not however trust to any one, but look after it yourself, and never let the carriage stand in the hot sun, as this will blister the pannels and cause the paint to fall off; neither let any persons get up behind when you are out with it Always have small change with you to pay the gates, as the turnpike-man is not obliged to give any; and have a book in your pocket with a pencil to put down any thing you may pay for, as you may otherwise forget, and so be the loser by it. If, when you are out at any ladies' or gentlemen's houses, you are required to wait at table, be clean and smart for the honour of your employers and your own credit. You may learn something useful wherever you go if you pay attention. Take particular notice how the dinner is conducted, and if you should see any thing worth imitating adopt it. Never be too old to learn, but be thankful when told of any thing to your advantage or information. If you have to wait on your family when they dine on the road, endeavour to have things as you know they like them; if they should be stopping at a boarding-house, you will always have to wait on them when at dinner, and if there should be many families at the same house, you will find it a hard matter to get and keep your things for your family; as it is too often the case that servants will take each other's things at those places; endeavour, however, to have plenty of plates, knives and forks, and other things, and try to make every thing as comfortable as you are at home, for much depends on the attention of a servant at those places.

There is one thing, my young friends, which I wish to impress on your minds, as the neglect of it has been of very serious consequence to some: it is this; never *interfere* or *meddle* with other people's family matters, or their servants. Find no faults while from home, but put up with any little inconvenience rather than complain; keep yourself to yourself; and whatever you may hear or see, be *blind* and *dumb*, when any one wishes to know the secrets of the family you live with: this is both your duty and the safest plan to act on; and consider, that if, when you are from home, you have little, or even great difficulties to encounter, they are not of a nature to last, and that at any rate you have the pleasure of seeing different countries and manners to set against your care and fatigue.

If you travel with a single gentleman, be very particular in seeing about his bed-room, and likewise his dressing-room; try to make it as nearly like his own as you can; have his things well aired, and be careful when he has done dressing to put every thing in its proper place.

If at any time you should travel by the stage-coach to any place, do not satisfy inquisitive persons who may think proper to ask you who you live with, and all the particulars of your family. It is through servants doing this, that we hear of so many robberies and frauds, as thieves very often travel by stage-coaches. I once travelled with a person of this description from a watering-place, along with several other servants, of whom he had been very busily asking the particulars of their families, which they were incautious enough to satisfy him in, far more than they ought to have done. When he had got all he could out of them, he thought proper to address himself to me, saying, " Sir, I suppose your family are gone on before." I answered, " No, Sir." After a little pause, finding I did not say any thing more, he said, " I suppose you have left them behind;" to which I answered rather sharply, " No, Sir : *I left them on one side;*" looking him full in the face. To this I had no answer, nor any more questions; but my answer caused a little merriment to the rest of my fellow-travellers; for he

looked as if he felt the reproof.   In some such manner as this you may put inquisitive persons to silence,
without giving them a saucy answer, although they
richly deserve one.

WATERING-PLACES.

IF at any time you should go to a watering-place for
a few months with the family you live with, and
they should condescend to ask your opinion concerning the conveniences of the house they mean to
take, be very particular in seeing that there are
proper things for use, and if not, mention it before
the family go in ; have also the price of the glass and
other things set on them before you take it, as some
will want you (if any should be broken) to pay treble
its real value.   Look over the inventory of the things
before you use them, particularly the glass and china,
or any thing which is likely to be broken ; and see
that they are all sound and whole ; if any are cracked,
put them on one side, and show them to the person
who is with you when the inventory is looked over.
If there should be more things in the house than
what the family are likely to want, tell the person so,
and have them locked up, as a number of unnecessary things are only more trouble to account for ;
particularly steel knives and forks, which will soon
get rusty and be spoiled with the damp of the salt

L

water if not attended to. The tradesmen seem to be run wild at some of the watering-places, for they are after every person who comes like a pack of hounds in the chase after a fox, so that it makes it quite disagreeable for families to walk out for some time, they are beset so: this is what is called TOUTING. The Touters will promise also to do this or the other thing for the servants, if they will but speak for them; but turn a deaf ear to all their clamours, and recommend none on such principles. Look for those who have the best things, and sell on the most reasonable terms, and take no one for a constancy till *proved*. Never connive with a tradesman to rob your employers, as it is exceedingly wicked, and in the long-run you will find HONESTY is the best POLICY, and will give the greatest ease to the mind. There is another thing which honesty calls on you to observe; and that is, in all hired houses or lodgings, to be as careful of the furniture and things you have to use, as though they were your employer's, or your own. It is cruel to do otherwise, as the persons who let them have in general been servants, or get their bread entirely by it.

Smuggling is much practised at watering-places, to the great injury of our own trade and countrymen, and sometimes to the injury of those who deal in it, as heavy fines are laid on those who are detected. Ladies and gentlemen have sometimes come to serious loss while travelling, through their servants having smuggled property about them;

for a single contraband article exposes the whole
of the property among which it is found to be
forfeited; therefore have nothing to do with it,
run no risk, but encourage our own trade, and
help to put bread in the mouths of our own countrymen instead of foreigners'. If ladies and gentlemen were to employ none but foreign servants,
what would become of us? We should not like it;
and indeed there are too many already kept in
families. Let us then, my young friends, refrain
from a practice which is contrary to the laws, and
injurious to the interests of our country, and cannot be entered into without meanness, falsehood,
and danger to ourselves.

SUNDRY THINGS WHICH OUGHT TO BE ATTENDED TO.

WHEN the winter begins to set in, cover the
water-pipes with hay or straw bands, twisted tight
round them. If it does not freeze at the time, let
the hay or straw be wet, as it will twist tighter in
that state, and it will soon get dry afterwards.
This is highly necessary to be attended to; for, if
you are short of water in a gentleman's house,
where there is so much wanted, you will find it
very distressing and inconvenient, and particularly
if you have to fetch it: therefore see to the pipes,
and water-buts, and cisterns, in time, to secure a
good supply.

In pumping up water into the cistern for the water-closet, you must be very particular in winter-time, as in general the pipes go up the outside of the house; in which case they are of course more likely to be frozen than if they were within. If then they go up the outside of the house, let all the water be let out of the pipe when you have done pumping; but if at any time you should forget to do so, and it should get frozen, take a small gimlet and bore a *hole* in the pipe, a little distance from the place where you let it off at, if the frost has not been so severe as to freeze all the water in the upper part of the pipe. By doing this you will prevent its bursting; and, at all events, it is the best way to do it so, as it will prevent the pipe bursting in more places than one. Have a peg to put into the hole after you have let the water off, and then you will only have to take it out at any time when the water may be frozen. Pump the water up into the cistern for the closet every morning, or as often as wanted, without waiting to be told, particularly if there be only ladies in the family where you live; and once a week, if the closet is where you can have free access to it, take a pail of water, and cast it into the basin, having first opened the pipe, that is, the trap which is at the bottom of the basin; this will clear the soil out of the pipe, and ought to be done at regular intervals.

You will find it necessary at times to clear and sweep the footway before the house, particularly in winter, to remove the snow from the pavement; this should be done as soon as possible, not only to prevent accidents, but to spare your master or mistress a fine, which they are liable to if it be not done in proper time. If at any time there should be a great fall of snow, it perhaps will be necessary to have it taken from off the top of the house; if so, you must be careful not to use any thing which may cut holes in the leaden gutter or leads at the top of the house. This kind of work is, however, seldom required of servants, as there is great danger in doing it to persons who are not accustomed to such things; but still you ought to see that those who do it are persons whom you can trust, and that know their business; for, if not, they may do a great deal of damage to the leads. If the snow should be frozen on a sky-light, let none attempt to brush it off, for, if they do, they will most likely break every glass in so doing.

CONCERNING WORKMEN.

If at any time you should live in a family where there should be workmen employed in repairing the house, be careful that you leave nothing of plate about to tempt them, as many of them are very dishonest; therefore put every thing out of their way, and trust to none, although several may be honest: but this you cannot tell till you try them, and it is too late when things are lost to be careful.

Likewise have as little to say to them as you possibly can, and never tell them any thing concerning the family, as many houses have been robbed through servants doing this; therefore keep them at a proper distance. Behave with civility to them, this is required of you; but give no orders to them, nor take any from them, further than a message to your employers, unless you are authorized to do more by those whom you serve.

MAKING UP THE FIRE.

As in the drawing-rooms and parlours you will have the fires to attend to when once they are lighted, be careful, in taking the coal-scuttle into the rooms, that you do not run against the chairs, or any thing else, to scatter the coals about the room. Throw up the cinders from under the grate before you put the coals on, then sweep up the hearth and fire-place neatly; but if there be any part of the company sitting near the fender, do not sweep so that the dust will fly over them. Whenever you go into the rooms, and see that the fires want making up, do it without being told, unless ordered to the contrary.

TAPPING THE BEER.

Always have the beer-cock well washed before you put it into the cask, and only use wood to drive it in with, for, if you take any thing which is iron for that purpose, you will most likely break the cock in so doing. Have the vent-peg loose while you tap it, if it has not been loosened for some time before; this will prevent its flying about. If the cock goes hard, put a little sweet-oil to it, which will make it turn easily, and put some paper round it, to make it fit properly, so that the beer shall not leak out. When it requires tilting, let it be done while it is running; this will prevent it getting thick. If you cannot do it yourself, have a person to assist you: of course, you will have a proper tilt for that purpose.

HOLYDAY-MAKING.

If at any time you get leave to go out to see your friends, be very particular that you do not stay beyond the time which may have been allotted you. Pay great attention to this, and rather be home before, than stop five minutes after it; by doing this you will gain the good-will of the family; never ask for leave to go out, if you can any way help it, when you have reason to suspect that you may be particularly wanted, as some ladies and gentlemen, rather than disappoint you, may be kind enough to let you go, even though they cannot spare you without inconvenience to themselves.

IMPROVEMENT OF TIME.

THERE are, my young friends, many ways wherein you may employ your time, so as to turn it to good advantage to yourselves and those round about you. You must consider that you may not be always in service, as many things may prevent this even if you wished it: you will do well, therefore, to turn your mind to the future, and ask yourselves a few questions, such as these: " What should I do if not in service?"—" What am I fit for if I leave service?" or, " How can I get my bread when I leave service?" If there is no particular thing which your mind may be impressed with, or have in view, you will do well to improve yourselves in general knowledge; but if you have any thing which you may intend to enter into when you leave service, pay the more attention to this, that you may be proportionally fitted for it when opportunity offers. I shall observe a few things concerning the many ways in which you may improve your time; for in some families you will have a great deal of it on your hands, while in others you perhaps will have but little. Remember, however, that we are ordered in all cases to redeem the time, for our *days* are but *few*.

The first thing I wish to impress on your mind

is the study of the Bible, by which you may learn your duty to God, your neighbour, and yourselves; learn the divine and blessed precepts of our great Benefactor; see what commands he has given unto us for our good here, and our eternal happiness hereafter; which if you read and practise, you will be established in your duty towards God and your neighbour, and this will prepare your mind for every other kind of knowledge that will be of any service to you in your situation of life. Let this divine knowledge be the foundation or touchstone to which you will bring all other knowledge in subserviency; let it have the pre-eminence in your affections and desire, as it will be to each of you what the ballast is to a ship, for all other knowledge, if this is wanting, will bring you no real happiness, but will puff you up with pride, and be a torment to you, while the knowledge of religion will be like a kind and affectionate father, who will say to you, "My son, give not thyself to strong drink, to whoring, to theft, pride, foolishness, cruelty, deceit, and idleness; turn away from those things which only bring with them disgrace and death." He will likewise reason with you and say, "Wherefore do you spend your money and strength for that which satisfieth not? but incline your ear and come unto me, and buy *wisdom*, *wine*, and *milk*, and heavenly blessings, without money and without price."—Isaiah, xlv.; St. James, iii. This is the true wisdom and knowledge which cometh from above, and will be a guide unto all other, and be like a wise preceptor in all your pursuits through life, if you adhere to its injunctions.

The next things which I could wish you to improve yourselves in, are grammar and arithmetic; without a little of these to direct you in writing and keeping accounts, you will not be able to hold any situation of credit, nor indeed a place as a servant in any trust, as you may have to write to your employers, when they may be from home, on business; therefore it is quite necessary to know how to express yourselves that you may be understood : besides, many ladies and gentlemen have been prevented from bettering the situation of their servants through their ignorance, and want of a little knowledge in arithmetic and writing; therefore, my young friends, pay particular attention to both, as they will be highly necessary if you enter into any kind of business; indeed, you can be in no situation where they will not be of use to you, as it is always a pleasure to a person to be able to write and cast up accounts well.

The next thing to improve your mind in will be a little knowledge of the history of our own country. Look over the different counties, and notice the particular trades or manufactures which each county is noted for, or any thing peculiar in its nature, soil, or produce; look back in history, and see what ignorance and barbarism covered the people of this now happy land a few ages ago; compare that time with the present, see what a difference in point of civilization and cultivation ; see what a gradual rise of the arts and sciences within a few hundred years past; and what blessings and comforts we have now to what the people had in good KING ALFRED's time.   By reading the history of your own nation, you will be fitted to read that of others, if you have leisure ; this you can do at a small expense, by providing yourself with a book on geography, a gazetteer, and a small dictionary of arts and sciences : those will cost you very little, and you will be enabled by them to look as it were into other kingdoms, states, and countries, by your quiet fireside ; you will see the various machines, tools, and instruments, which are used in the different trades, and the various productions of na ture, and indeed every thing which is remarkable in the world.   In making this a part of your study, you will gain a fund of agreeable information to talk of when in company, instead of exposing the secrets of the family you live with, or the faults of your fellow-servants and acquaintances, or those of your own relations, as many do for want of knowing any better subjects of conversation. You may read books of this kind while at home in your duty, as you need never be ashamed of any body seeing you so employed, and they will often render you an additional service by keeping you out

of bad company and from a public-house, as well as
by improving your mind.

There is another way of gaining a great deal of
useful knowledge, which may often be of service to
yourself, and likewise to those whom you serve—I
mean the newspaper; but I do not mean that part
which treats on politics and the administering of public
affairs : this is what we servants have. but little to
do with, or at least ought not to have, as we have
neither learning nor judgment sufficiently informed
to speak of these things with propriety and accu-
racy ; besides, politics are above our sphere of life,
from which we cannot expect any good to be done
by our talents, even admitting we may have some ;
but much harm may be done, and has been done,
through servants debating on politics, the peace of
many families having been broken through the con-
tending parties, for, as it is very seldom that persons who are so fond of talking politics have wisdom
to argue and speak deliberately on them, it often
ends in a quarrel, if not with *blows*. On this account many families prohibit debating on politics ;
and they are wise in so doing, as the peace of the
servants may be broken through it, and we are
sure no good can be done by it. Much better
would it be to society at large, if servants and
tradesmen would employ their time and ability in
their own business, and in trying to make their
homes more comfortable for themselves and their
families, than in going to a public-house at nights

to debate on politics. We should not in that case see so many *bankrupts*, or so many *paupers* on the parish; but it is now unfortunately quite common for tradesmen and servants to have their regular rendezvous, where they meet to debate on politics, and to arraign His Majesty's ministers before them, as it were, and pass their judgment on them with all the assurance possible, without an IF or a BUT, and talk how they would do this, that, and the other thing, if they had but the managing of the affairs of the nation; yet those very persons cannot manage their own with credit to themselves and comfort to their families. Be careful that you are not drawn into those parties under the idea of being a select company, &c. and having a private room to yourselves: this has been the means of enticing many who would never have thought of going to a public-house if they had not been drawn into it this way, but who by going a few times got acquainted with various persons, and liked the proceedings, and at last could not feel happy unless they were in the same sort of company every night, which has been the complete ruin of them and their families. My young friends, you will find it an easy matter to get acquaintance and bad habits, but it will be a hard matter to get rid of either.

Having cautioned you against what you are to avoid in the papers; I shall proceed to point out what is most worthy of notice in them. Be particular in reading the police accounts, accidents, and the trials at the different assizes: from these and things of the like nature you will gain much useful information that you may profit by; for instance, you will often see in the police reports accounts of *swindlers, robbers,* and *duffers,* and the various ways they have contrived and made use of to defraud; this will put you on your guard not to be so taken in: and sometimes you will see an account of a servant bringing an action against his master for insult or false character, which will be a hint to you never to take the law into your own hands when insulted and ill-treated, and remind you that the law takes cognizance of a master's ill conduct as well as of a servant's: and you will now and then read of a dishonest servant being apprehended and brought to justice for his bad conduct; this will admonish you not to do the same thing, or any thing like it, which can cause you to fall into such disgrace: and, under the article Accidents, you will see what evil has befallen some persons through neglect and inattention: and now and then you will find some useful receipts, that may be of great service to you, or those whom you may serve; in such a case always write them down, which will both impress them on your mind and improve you in writing. You may likewise notice on the trials some particular *points* of *law,* which it may be useful to you as well as to your employers to bear in mind, as it has often happened that servants, through carelessness and ignorance, have done things which have been illegal, and thus they have undesignedly involved their employers in a lawsuit. Make it your study to improve by what you read; but do not, in your eagerness to do so, keep the paper back from your employers, to read it before they have had it, but wait till they have done with it before you attempt to look at it. Some families will not let their servants read the newspaper at all; but this has been almost always owing to their disputing on *politics*, which I hope will never be your case.

If at any time some of you should be left in town, or at the country-house, when the family may be on a visit, or any where else from home, for a few weeks or months, this will give you a great opportunity of improving yourself in reading, or writing, or arithmetic, or any thing else. You will do well to put yourself under the tuition of a schoolmaster when you have a great deal of spare time; for, if you have not something to do, you will find it hang heavy on your hands, and you may be led into bad habits, such as gambling or loose company, for want of better employment.

I hope, my young friends, you will not be frequenters of public-houses; they are useful in their way, but not a fit place to go to for amusement and to spend your time and money, as you seldom hear any thing in them but profane and wicked conversation, which can only fit the mind for some bad end. I hope you will likewise abstain from the reading of blasphemous and licentious books, as they are to the mind of man what poison is to his body; they will speedily corrupt all your best feelings and principles, and both fit and lead you on to unhappiness, and finally to destruction; therefore ponder your ways in your own mind, and ask yourself if you are pursuing the path that will lead to peace and honour. I am sure, if you will contrast the life of a man who is a frequenter of public-houses and bad company, with one who is staying at home and minding his business, you will be constrained to say, this man who stays at home is the happiest, for he is a credit to himself, a comfort to those round about him, and an honour to his situation; leading a holy life, which will insure him a *comfortable death* and a prospect of a better world. This is the only character that enjoys this present world; the profane and wicked do not, for they have it, but enjoy it not: they desire and have it not, as they seek happiness where it is not to be found.

RELIGION.

To be diligent in business is what our religion as well as our own interest requires of us; but this alone will not give us any real pleasure at the thought of meeting our Lord and Judge at the last day of account, as there are many very dili-

gent and clever in business who are likewise the
most abandoned persons possible, and will give
themselves up to work all manner of wickedness;
and yet they will have the good name of some,
because they are said to *take care of the main
chance;* and a poor chance it will be if this is all
they care about. I know some will exclaim, What
is religion? Indeed, what is it? If it means, as
some think it does, to *reconsider,* that is, to reflect on our actions and conduct towards God and
our neighbour, some would do well to do so before
it is too late: but, my young friends, I trust most
of you know what is meant by religion, and to the
rest, who do not, I shall say what I understand
it to be, which is this: to practise what God
has commanded and enjoined us to do; to love him
with all our heart, and our neighbour as ourselves
(that is, to do unto others as we should wish they
should unto us, if we were in their situation and
they in ours); to love all virtue and hate all vice;
and to be often reading the GOOD BOOK, THE BIBLE,
wherein is a system of laws and commands to regulate our conduct towards God and our fellow-
creatures, with promises to encourage us in love
and obedience. This is what I understand by religion and being religious; and I trust the good
hand of the Lord will be with each of you, that
you may be enabled to walk in his ways blameless;
in doing which you will find more true comfort
and peace of mind than in any thing else: this

will make a death-bed easy, and we shall leave this world with a joyful prospect of another far better. It is, my young friends, to the Bible and the diffusion of the sacred laws, precepts, and principles which it contains, that we are more indebted for being happy and civilized than any other nation under the sun. Only take a view of the places where the Bible is not known, or not allowed to be read, and you will see that the greatest cruelty and ignorance debase the human mind. Yes, my young friends, where the Bible is not attended to there is little else than oppression, cruelty, and a wish to tyrannize over each other; but if the Bible is read, and its sacred principles followed, the weakest is as safe as the strongest, the poor as the rich, for the laws and commands of God have no respect to persons: what is sin in one is sin in the other, if he doth the same action. The different stations in life are appointed by God, and happiness is not peculiar to any of them, not to rank and riches any more than in having only just enough to satisfy our daily wants: indeed happiness does not consist in the things of this world any farther than as we receive them for the glory of God and the welfare of our fellow-creatures: thus by using and not abusing this world's goods, we shall enjoy them to the glory of God and our own comfort.

Now, consider there is no true happiness here unless it has God for its author; and if we wish to find it we must seek it in the way where God has placed it. The Bible is the only book that shows us the way; then let us make its commands and precepts our daily study, with prayer unto the Lord, that he would give us wisdom to understand and a willing heart to obey its dictates. Attend public worship with reverence; be zealous in your walk and conversation to promote the honour of God and the welfare of his people. Do nothing rashly, but well consider every thing before you act. In the Bible you will find promised to those who ask aright, *eyes to the blind, wisdom to the foolish, health to the sickly, strength to the weak, ears to the deaf, riches to the poor, encouragement to the fearful, and even life, from everlasting death and destruction,* THROUGH *our* LORD *and* SAVIOUR JESUS CHRIST. But remember, this book also commands us to act uprightly in all our dealings, to speak the truth, to be obedient to all in authority over us, to be diligent in business, to be merciful to the poor, and to do them good as far as in us lies; to guide the strayed sheep, when found, back into the fold; to help the weak, to instruct the ignorant, and those who are out of the right way, in meekness and humility, as remembering that we ourselves are in the *flesh* and subject to frailties.

Now, my young friends, if you happen to live with those who may profess a faith or mode of worship different from your own, remember that in essential things you most likely have still the same opinions. You all acknowledge but one God, one Saviour, one faith, one hope, one object in view, which is the glory of God and your own and your fellow-creatures' happiness. You acknowledge God to be the great Protector and universal Father of us all, and the Bible the only book you wish to be ruled by and take your articles of faith from. Do not, then, fall out on your way to heaven, and charge each other with erroneous doctrines and damnable principles; learn Christian moderation toward each other, and if you only differ in mere form of worship, let not this be a bone of contention among you; for, consider whatever you may think of another, that same person may in return think of you, as I have no doubt but each of you will think your own way the best; this is natural enough; but, my young friends, if any of you wish to show the superiority of his principles, let it be by a better walk and conversation in holiness, rather than in noisy wrangling disputations: for, consider, "God is love," and Christ is the "Prince of peace;" then how inconsistent must it be for you to fall out and reproach each other, who call yourselves the children of God, and of course are brethren in Christ! Remember what Joseph said to his brethren; he commanded them not to fall out by the way home: so I exhort you likewise, for consider how many enemies and blasphemers of the Bible and our holy religion there are to contend with; therefore do not attempt to get the better of each other, or any one else, as religion does not consist in outward forms, for, to worship God aright, is to worship him in spirit and in truth, to obey his commands and keep his precepts, and do unto others that which we would wish them to do unto us, were we in their situation and they in ours. Consider that the honour of God and the comfort of our fellow-creatures and ourselves are not promoted by a persecuting spirit; see what our dear Lord said to his disciples; how sharply he rebuked their unchristian spirit toward those who did not go about with them in his day; they wanted fire from heaven to consume them; but he rebukes them, and tells them that they knew not what manner of spirit they were of. St. Mark, chap. ix. ver. 38, 39. Make it, therefore, my young friends, a matter of prayer unto God to direct your steps aright; remember the Lord exhorts you to the unity of spirit, to lay aside all malice, strife, and persecution, and put on charity toward each other; for true religion and heavenly wisdom are *gentle, peaceable, easily* to be *entreated, full* of *good works,* and neither *speaking* nor *thinking ill.*

If, then, my young friends, Providence should place you in families of a different persuasion to your own, submit yourselves to the way and manner of those you live with, and attend public worship with them, if they wish it, provided they differ from you only in *form*, not in *principle;* if there is regular family prayer, attend to it with devotion, and show that you reverence the *solemn worship* by a respectful attention and a fit temper of mind. Do not expect perfection in this life in yourself or in any other, but try for it. Respect and reverence the ministers of the Lord, for they are his ambassadors of peace to publish glad tidings unto man; give them double honour for their work's sake; study the word of God, and hear what his ministers say; you will find it is like having an affectionate and kind father to admonish us when tempted to stray from the path of duty and peace. Provide yourself with a Bible; study it with humility and gratitude, and regulate all your thoughts, words, and actions by the precepts you will find written in it by the finger of God: you will then pass through life happy and respected, and meet death in the joyful hope of one who has made his calling sure, through the goodness of God, and the intercession of our blessed Guide and Pattern, as well as Lord and Saviour Jesus Christ.

ON CHANGING PLACES.

There is no doubt but that comfort and respectability generally accrue to servants in proportion to the length of time they stay in their places.

Circumstances, however, will arise which may occasion even the best servants to give up, or be deprived of a place; and therefore I wish to point out to you some considerations that you ought to bear in mind before entering on a new one. Recollect that frequent change is loss of time, loss of money, loss of character; therefore endeavour to ascertain both whether the place be fit for you, and whether you be fit for the place; what there is to do, and what will be expected from you, and likewise whether the family have any particular ways or rules that they may wish to have observed.

Sometimes, when servants have got into a place and their new clothes are made, they have thought proper to give warning to leave; this is very unbecoming behaviour and also unjust, unless a satisfactory cause can be assigned for so doing; therefore never have your new clothes till you see whether you suit the place and the place you; if the family insist on your having them, this will not be your fault, only never think of changing your situation for trifles. Remember, that in all places you will have something to put up with, and consider well before you give warning, whether you may find one that will suit you better, or indeed one of any kind, in a reasonable time. If you leave your situation merely on account of having low wages, consider how long you may be without any wages at all, but spending what you have already got; for a few pounds go but a little way when you have every thing to buy, and your clothes are all wearing out. Never give warning while in a passion, or when you have done wrong and may have been chided for it.

Even should your family at any time ill-treat or find fault with you unjustly, you must consider they have their troubles to put them out of temper, and a servant may lose a good place through taking notice of such things; but if you have reason to think they have taken a dislike to you, give them proper warning, and leave them, for you cannot be comfortable in a family where you do not give satisfaction. When you go after a place, be clean in your dress and respectful in your behaviour; do not speak with an air of self-importance, or answer impertinently to any thing which you do not approve of; state your objections coolly, and let your arguments be reasonable. Never, if you can do without, take a place which is only for a short time, or *a job* as it is called, for this is no recommendation to a servant. Always inquire into the character of the family in which you are trying to procure a situation, as you may get into some from which no respectable people will take a character afterwards; and not only this, but you may get a place in which you may not be able to stop, as some do not allow their servants common necessary things to do their work with, or provisions to satisfy their appetites, which is every way unjust, as the labourer is worthy of his hire. As to your wages, you must consider, that when you are old no one will hire you; it is only while you are young and active, and able to run about, that you are valued; therefore it is necessary to have wages to enable you to put by a few pounds against you want it. You ought to calculate what your clothes and washing will cost you; and then you will be enabled to form an idea of what you can save. You will find, on a moderate calculation, that, to keep yourself neat and clean, your washing will cost you about seven pounds a year; mending, one more; linen, four pounds; shoes, two pounds; tea and sugar, four pounds: this makes all together eighteen pounds a year, that you will have to lay out on yourself in indispensable necessaries. If you are with a family that keep you waiting, as some do, for hours in the streets, you will have an additional source of expense, in being sometimes obliged, in wet or cold weather, to go under shelter, and have a glass of something; though I would advise you never to do it but when you are afraid of doing harm to your health, or your clothes, by getting wet.

In many families they allow the men-servants one shilling a night if they are out after a certain hour, to enable them to get something; indeed, in some places the footmen and coachmen are out for weeks together every night till a late hour, standing in the cold and wet streets: you should take this

into consideration in going after situations. Where a
servant is always out, or travelling about, and often
in hotels, he cannot help spending something, let
him be ever so careful; therefore a quiet place,
where you are not exposed to the foregoing tempt-
ations, will be better in the long run, even if you
have a pound or two less wages than in the other;
and particularly for your health, as, to be up late and
exposed to the damp and cold air, and your rest
broken at nights, is very injurious to any one, and
particularly to gentlemen's servants, who are used
at home to such hot rooms and great fires, and then
have to go and stand in the street for hours, which
has caused many a long and painful disease ending
in death. Always have thick shoes, and be well
clothed, when you go out with the carriage in the
evening, or have to stand about in the damp streets:
this may prevent a fit of illness, which might de-
prive you for months of the means of getting your
bread. When you have got a few pounds in service, put it in the Bank; this will get more. The
Savings Banks, which have been established of late
years, are the best and most convenient for servants,
as you can put in a few shillings at a time; and if
you should be removed by Providence from the
place where you have put your money in, you will
not have any cause to be running backward and
forward to take the interest of it, unless you should
be in want of it; for, by leaving it, you will get
compound interest for it. Always ask for your

money every half-year: if you do not particularly want it, you may as well put it in the Savings Bank, and get a few shillings. Never let your money lie in your employer's hands year after year, as many have done to their sorrow. Some ladies and gentlemen have been kind enough to allow their servants interest on their money which they have retained in their hands, but this is very unsafe; several whom I know, after having lived in a family for twenty, nay, one for thirty years, and having only taken just enough of their wages to buy them common necessary things from their employers, and left all the rest in their hands, expecting to have something to make their old age comfortable, have found, to their unspeakable disappointment and distress both of body and mind, the master or mistress whom they have served all the prime of their days, has either died without mentioning them, or lived beyond their income, so that they could not refund the money which was their servants' due: the principal and interest thus both lost, the poor aged, and almost worn-out servants have been turned out, with an enfeebled body, a perplexed mind, and broken-down spirit, to begin the world afresh. This is a truly heart-rending sight, particularly when we consider that if those persons had put their money in the Bank, they would have had enough to make them comfortable the few remaining days they had to live, but now must know want, and perhaps die in the poor-house. However fair the promises of your employers may be, trust not in *man* any more than you can help; therefore, when you have a little money to put by, lodge it in the Bank. There is another thing which I will warn you against, that is, in lending out your money with the intent to get double interest, or nearly so. Some have got a great deal by so doing, while others have lost both interest and principal too. Many will lend out their money to young gentlemen under age, because they will give great interest for it; but, remember this is illegal, and you must rely solely on the honour of the person to whom you lend it, whether you ever have either interest or principal again; and how much you may depend on the honour of most of those gentlemen, I will leave others to tell you who have tried them to their sorrow. However specious an opportunity may offer itself to you to lend your money out, remember, man is but man, in his best estate full of vanity and deceptions: I do not say all are alike, as many gentlemen have done good for their servants, in keeping their money for them; but many have failed, and cheated them out of both principal and interest; while, in the Bank, not an instance can be given of wronging a person of either; and a moderate and sure interest is much better than an uncertain one, although ever so high. Be contented, therefore, with ease of mind, security, and the BANK.

APPENDIX:

VARIOUS USEFUL RECEIPTS AND TABLES.

To make Blacking.—Vide p. 16.

TAKE four ounces of ivory black, three ounces of coarse brown sugar, and a table-spoonful of sweet oil, and mix them gradually together in a pint of cold small beer.

To render Shoes water-proof.

Mix a pint of drying oil, two ounces of yellow wax, two ounces of turpentine, and half an ounce of Burgundy pitch, carefully over a slow fire. Lay the mixture whilst hot on the boots or shoes, with a sponge or soft brush; and when they are dry lay it on again, and again, until the leather becomes quite saturated, that is to say, will hold no more. Let them then be put away, and not be worn until they are perfectly dry and elastic; they will afterwards be found not only impenetrable to wet, but soft and pliable, and of much longer duration.

To prevent Snow-water from penetrating Boots or Shoes.

Take equal quantities of bees wax and mutton suet, and melt them together in an earthen pipkin, over a slow fire. Lay the mixture whilst hot on the boots and shoes, which ought to be made warm also; let them stand before the fire a short time, for it to soak in, and then put them away, until they are quite cold. When they are so, rub them dry with a piece of flannel, in order that you may not grease your blacking brushes.

M 3

If you black them well, before you put the mixture on, you will find them take the blacking much better afterwards. Do not put either oil or wax on leather *alone*; oil opens the pores of it too much, and wax causes it to crack.

To clean Boot-tops white.

Take an ounce of oxalic acid, dissolve it in a pint of soft water, and keep it in a bottle well corked; dip a soft sponge into the mixture to clean the tops with, and if there be any spots which refuse to disappear, rub them with a little fine Bath brick dust; sponge the tops afterwards with clean water. Take particular care always to have any mixtures, or powders for boot-tops, labelled with the word POISON in large letters, as the most dreadful accidents have arisen from oxalic acid, being so like Epsom salts in appearance, as to be often taken for them in mistake, and also from the burning nature of vitriol, which is another ingredient much used in cleaning boot-tops.

To clean Boot-tops brown.

Take a pint of skimmed milk, half an ounce of spirits of salt, half an ounce of spirits of lavender, one ounce of gum arabic, and the juice of two lemons; mix them all well together, and keep them in a bottle closely corked; rub the tops with a sponge, but use no brick-dust; and when they are dry, polish them with a brush or a piece of flannel.

Plate Powder.—Vide p. 29.

Rouge powder, which is an excellent thing for cleaning plate, is sold ready prepared at various shops. Another safe and expeditious way of cleaning plate is as follows:

Boil an ounce of prepared hartshorn-powder in a quart of water. While on the fire put as much plate (well cleaned from grease and dirt) into it as the vessel will hold; let it boil a little time, then take it out, drain it over the saucepan, dry it before the fire, and rub it bright with leather. Then put more into the pan in the same manner until it is all boiled. Put clean linen rags into the pan to soak up the remainder, and when dry, they will give a beautiful polish to the plate merely by rubbing it with them. They are likewise admirable for the cleaning of brass locks, and the finger-plates of doors.

Another Way.

Melt an ounce of zinc in an iron ladle, then put two ounces of quicksilver to it; turn the mixture out on paper, pound it very fine, and then mix it with two pounds of the best whitening carefully sifted, and half an ounce of vermilion; pound them all together, and apply them as directed under the head of Cleaning Plate; and you will find them give a most beautiful polish to it. The quicksilver being killed by mixing it with the zinc, will no way injure the plate.

To clean plated Articles.

Take an ounce of killed quicksilver, which you may buy at the chymists', and half a pound of the best whitening sifted; mix them with spirits of wine when used.

To clean Mahogany Furniture.—Vide p. 36.

Mix one ounce of litharge with one quart of cold-drawn linseed oil; place them near the fire for ten days, shaking them occasionally; then lay it on the furniture for a day or two, if you have an opportunity; rub it off dry, and polish with clean cloths.

Another Way.

Mix four pennyworth of alkanet and two pennyworth of rose-pink in a pint of cold-drawn linseed oil; let them stand all night in an earthen vessel, then rub the mixture, after stirring it, on the tables; let it lie some time, then rub them dry, and polish them with linen cloths.

Varnish for Furniture.

Melt one part of virgin white wax in eight parts of oil of petroleum. Lay a slight coat of this mixture while warm on the wood with a badger's brush, and after a little time polish it with a coarse woollen cloth.

German Polish for Furniture.

Melt a quarter of a pound of yellow wax and an ounce of black resin, well beaten in an earthen pipkin. Then pour in by degrees two ounces of spirits of turpentine. When the whole is thoroughly mixed, put it into an earthen jar, and keep it covered for use. Spread a little of it on the furniture with a woollen cloth, rub it well in, and in a few days the polish will be as hard and bright as varnish.

To clean Brass Ornaments.—Vide p. 39.

Brass ornaments, when not gilt or lackered, may be cleaned with emery and oil mixed together, and laid on with a brush, or soft piece of wood. They may likewise have a brilliancy equal to that of gold given to them by either of the following simple processes. Beat sal ammoniac into a fine powder; rub it, moistened with soft water, on the ornaments, which must be heated over charcoal, and then rubbed dry with bran and whitening. Or wash the brass work with roche alum boiled in strong lye, in the proportion of an ounce to a pint; and when dry rub it with fine tripoli.

To take Stains out of Scarlet Cloth.—Vide p. 45.

Take soap wort, bruise it, strain out the juice, and add to it a small quantity of black soap; wash the stains a few times with this liquor, suffering it to dry between whiles, and in a day or two they will disappear.

To take Stains out of Black Cloth, Silk, Crape, &c.

Boil a large handful of fig-leaves in two quarts of water until reduced to a pint. Squeeze the leaves, and put the liquor into a bottle for use. The articles need only be rubbed with a sponge, dipped in the liquor, and the stains will instantly disappear.

To take Grease Spots out of Silk.

Dip a clean piece of flannel into spirits of turpentine, and rub the spots until they disappear, which will soon be the case. Do not be sparing of the turpentine, as it will all evaporate, and leave no mark or stain behind.

Varnish for old Straw or Chip Hats.—Vide p. 51.

Take half an ounce of the best black sealing-wax, bruise it and put it to two ounces of spirit of turpentine; melt them very gently, by placing the bottle that holds them in boiling water, or near a fire. When all the wax is melted, lay it on warm with a fine hair brush near the fire or in the sun. It will not only give a beautiful gloss and stiffness to the hats, but make them resist wet.

Wash for Leather Gloves.—Vide p. 52.

If you wish to have your gloves quite yellow, take yellow ochre; if quite white, pipe-clay; if between the two, mix a little of each together; if dark, take rotten stone and fuller's earth. By proper mixture of these you may produce any shade you desire; mix the colour you fix on with beer or vinegar, not water, and apply it as before directed.

To clean Gold and Silver Lace.

Sew the lace in linen cloth, boil it in a pint of water and two ounces of soap, and then wash it in water. When it is tarnished apply a little warm spirits of wine to the tarnished place.

To clean gilt Buckles, Chains, &c.

Dip a soft brush in water, rub a little soap on it, and brush the article for a minutue or two, then wash it clean, wipe it, and place it near the fire till dry, then brush it with burnt bread finely powdered.

To manage Razor Strops.—Vide p. 54.

Keep them moderately moist with a drop or two of sweet oil: a little crocus martis and a few drops of sweet oil, rubbed well in with a glass bottle, will give the razor a fine edge; pass it afterwards on the inside of your hand when warm, and dip it in hot water just before using.

To preserve Clothes from Moths, &c.

Put cedar shavings, or chippings of Russia leather, among the drawers and shelves where the clothes are kept. Pieces of camphor, or of tallow candle, wrapt up in paper, will preserve furs and woollens from moths; and lavender, roses, and flowers, and perfumes of every kind, are useful as well as agreeable in keeping away moths and worms.

To clean japanned Tea and Coffee Urns.—Vide p. 68.

Take an ounce of crocus powder and half an ounce of rotten stone, pound them well together; let the mixture be a little darker than the urn: you need not use rotten stone if you can get the crocus powder dark enough. Rub the urns with this powder as directed for plate.

To mix a Salad.—Vide p. 88.

Always inquire, before you mix a salad, how your master or mistress would like to have it done. If no particular method be pointed out to you, adopt the following, which has been much approved of. Let the salad be well washed and dried in a cloth before you cut it up; save a part of the celery with a little beet-root and endive for ornament in the middle of the dish: cut the rest small as well as the lettuce and mustard and cresses, and put to it the following mixture: take the yolk of an egg boiled hard, rub it quite smooth with a table-spoonful of oil and a little mustard; when they are well mixed together add six spoonfuls of milk or cream, and when they are well mixed put six or seven spoonfuls of vinegar to the whole and mix it all together with the salad. Never make the salad long before it is wanted, as it becomes flat with standing.

To make Toast and Water.

Take a thin slice of stale bread, toast it a deep brown on both sides, but do not burn or blacken it; put it into a deep jug and fill the jug up with boiling water, cover it and let it stand until cold. Some prefer cold water, in which case somewhat more time for it to stand is necessary. Always inquire which is most agreeable, and let it be strained through a fine and perfectly clean sieve, before you take it up stairs.

To make Punch.

One tea-spoonful of Coxwell's acid salt of lemons; a quarter of a pound of sugar, a quart of boiling water, half a pint of rum, and a quarter of a pint of brandy; add a little lemon-peel, if agreeable, or a drop or two of essence of lemon.

To make Ginger Beer.

Take an ounce of powdered ginger, half an ounce of cream of tartar, a large lemon sliced, two pounds of lump sugar, and one gallon of water; mix all together, and let it simmer over the fire for half an hour, then put a table-spoonful of yeast to it, let it ferment a little time, and then put it into stone pint bottles, and cork it down closely for use.

To make Spruce Beer.

Take eight gallons of boiling water, and add it to eight gallons of cold. Mix with it sixteen pounds of treacle or molasses, six table-spoonfuls of essence of spruce, and half a pint of yeast. Keep it in a temperate situation with the bung-hole open, two days, then close up the cork, or bottle it off, and it will be fit to drink in a few days afterwards.

To make Coffee.—Vide p. 112.

To two ounces of the best coffee, fresh ground, put eight coffee-cups of boiling water, let it boil six minutes, pour out a cupful two or three times, and return it again; then put two or three isinglass chips or a few hartshorn shavings into it, and pour one large spoonful of boiling water on it: boil it five minutes more, and let the pot stand by the fire ten minutes, for the coffee to settle. It will then be clear and bright. If it is wished to be particularly strong, three ounces of coffee must be used for eight cups; and if it is not fresh roasted, let it be made perfectly hot and dry, before or over the fire, before it is used. A tea-spoonful of the best mustard flour added to every ounce of coffee, greatly improves it, both in clearness and flavour. Serve hot milk or cream with it, and pounded sugar-candy or fine Lisbon sugar.

To cure ropy Beer.—Vide p. 222.

When beer turns ropy without being sour, it is easily restored by mixing in the proportion of one spoonful of mustard to every fourteen gallons, in a little of the beer, and pouring it into the bung-hole. In the course of the next day the beer will be fit for use. When it is actually sour it may be restored by hanging a linen bag in the cask, with equal quantities of pounded chalk and calcined oyster-shells. This will cure it in the space of a day and a night, but it will not keep very long after these additions.

Excellent Substitute for Table Beer.

In warm weather more table beer is wasted, by turning sour, than drank. The following mixture will be found a cheap and agreeable substitute for it. To ten quarts of water put a bottle of porter and a pound of brown sugar or treacle; add a spoonful of powdered ginger if the flavour of it be approved. When the whole is well mixed together put it into bottles, cork them loosely, place them in a cool cellar, and in two or three days it will be fit to drink.

To try the Goodness of Spirits.

Set fire to some in a spoon; if good, it will burn brightly away without leaving any moisture behind.

To know whether a Bed be damp or not.

After the bed is warmed put a glass goblet in between the sheets, and if the bed be damp, in a few minutes drops of wet will appear in the inside of the glass. This is of great consequence to be attended to in travelling, as many persons have laid the foundation of incurable and fatal disorders by sleeping in a damp bed.

On warming Beds.

Take all the black or blazing coals out of the pan, and scatter a little salt over the remainder, which will prevent the smell of sulphur, so disagreeable to delicate persons.

On mending Fires.

When you sweep up the hearth, lay a shovelfull of the dirt and ashes from under the grate upon the fire, and then a shovelfull of fresh coals, and so on alternately, until the grate is full, leaving room for a few large coals in front. This kind of fire will burn longer and brighter than if made of coals alone, causes less smoke, and leaves very little waste.

Remedy against Fleas.

Sew the leaves of fresh pennyroyal in little muslin bags, and put them between the blankets or mattresses. Wormwood or dried moss will have the same effect.

To prevent being Bug-bitten.

Put a sprig or two of tansey at the bed head, or as near the pillow as the smell may be agreeable.

To destroy Bugs.

Take six pennyworth of bitter apple dissolved in a pint of water, and wash the joints and crevices of the bedstead with it. Spirits of turpentine will have the same effect, as will also common mercurial ointment.

To kill Flies.

Dissolve two drachms of extract of quassia in half a pint of boiling water, sweeten it, and pour it into plates to be set about the room. This mixture, though fatal to the flies, is not injurious to any thing else, as most fly-waters are.

To destroy Rats or Mice.

Bait your traps with flour of malt mixed up into little balls, with butter, and scented with a drop or two of oil of anise-seed.

To correct bad Smells.

Throw five or six pounds of quick lime, with a sufficient quantity of ashes or soapsuds, into the place affected.

To extinguish Fire in a Chimney.

Put a wet blanket over the whole of the front of the

fireplace; which will stop the current of air, and so extinguish the flames.

To bring Horses out of a Stable in case of Fire.

Throw the harness or saddle to which he may have been accustomed, over the back of a horse in this predicament, and he will come out of the stable as tractably as usual.

Fire Escape.

In all upper chambers there ought to be kept a stout rope which may be fastened at one end to any thing heavy in the room, and have a noose at the other, to facilitate the escape of children, or infirm persons; along the rope should be several large knots, placed at intervals as resting-places for the hands and feet of the person who drops down by it.

To cure Burns and Scalds.

Rub the part burnt every two or three hours with spirits of turpentine, or with vinegar if the skin be not broken, or vinegar and water cold. Half a pound of alum dissolved in a quart of water likewise makes an admirable wash for a burn or scald; bathe the part with a linen rag dipped in the mixture, then bind the rag upon it with a slip of linen, and keep it moist with the alum-water for two or three days without removing the bandage.

To cure a bruised Eye.

Take conserve of red roses and rotten apple in equal quantities, wrap them in a fold of thin cambric, or old linen, and apply it to the eye; it will relieve the bruise and remove the blackness.

To cure a sprained Ancle or Wrist.

Foment it with warm vinegar for five minutes every four hours, wet it afterwards with rectified spirits of wine, and rub it gently. Sit with the foot on a low stool, and occasionally rest upon the ancle, and move it gently backwards and forwards.

Remedy for a sore Throat.

Put some hot vinegar into an earthenware jug or tea-pot, and draw the steam through the spout or the pipe of a funnel; do it for about half an hour just before going to bed, also two or three times in the course of the day, provided you are not going out of doors: do not draw in the steam too suddenly at first, as you may in that case scald your throat. A piece of flannel dipped in hartshorn will be serviceable put round it on going to bed. In a relaxed sore throat a few lumps of sugar dipped in brandy, and gradually dissolved in the mouth, are very efficacious.

To make a saline Mixture.

Take a tea-spoonful of salt of wormwood, two tea-spoonfuls of cream of tartar, a few lumps of sugar, and a piece of lemon-peel, stir them together in a pint of cold water, and take a wine-glass full every two or three hours. If the mixture be too sour, add a little more salt of wormwood; if too salt, a little more cream of tartar. It is an admirable remedy in feverish complaints, and the quantity here prescribed may be made at home for twopence; whereas, if it came in due form, and labelled, from an apothecary's shop, it would cost eighteen-pence, or two shillings.

Cure for the Toothache.

The toothache attacks all descriptions of persons, and is a pain tormenting enough to try the patience even of those who have every advantage of quietness and indulgence, much more of such as are obliged to go about their work, and be exposed to all kinds of weather, alike when they are ill as when they are well. It is therefore highly desirable to know any thing that may lessen or cure a pain which may seize you at the very moment when you are most anxious to have all your faculties and vigour about you, for the performance of your duty. Different persons are affected by different things, according to their constitution, or the cause of their disorder. In some, the toothache may be cured by putting a piece of nut-gall into the hollow of the tooth, letting it stay half an hour or an hour, and then changing it for another, until the pain ceases.

In others a piece of lint dipped in laudanum with a few drops of oil of cloves, will have the same effect; and sometimes the oil left by a piece of writing paper burnt in a glass, will work a cure when put into the tooth, on a little cotton wool.

Acute Rheumatism.

Take a quarter of a pound of saltpetre, melt it near the fire in a quart of vinegar, and rub the part affected with it twice or three times a day, for about half an hour.

A Table of Priority or Precedency among Ladies; intended as a Guide to Servants in waiting on them, to serve them according to their respective Ranks.—Vide p. 123.

1. Daughters of the King.
2. Wives of the King's Sons.
3. Wives of the King's Brothers.
4. Wives of the King's Uncles.
5. Wives of the eldest Sons of Dukes of the blood royal.
6. Wives of the King's Nephews.
7. Wives of Archbishops.
8. Duchesses.
9. Marchionesses.
10. Wives of the eldest Sons of Dukes.
11. Daughters of Dukes.
12. Countesses.
13. Wives of the eldest Sons of Marquesses.
14. Daughters of Marquesses.
15. Wives of the younger Sons of Dukes.
16. Viscountesses.
17. Wives of the eldest Sons of Earls.
18. Daughters of Earls.
19. Wives of the younger Sons of Marquesses.
20. Wives of Bishops.
21. Baronesses.
22. Wives of the eldest Sons of Viscounts.
23. Daughters of Viscounts.
24. Wives of the younger Sons of Earls.
25. Wives of the Sons of Barons.
26. Maids of Honour.
27. Wives of the younger Sons of Viscounts.
28. Wives of the younger Sons of Barons.
29. Wives of Baronets.
30. Wives of Knights of the Garter.
31. Wives of Bannerets.
32. Wives of Knights Grand Crosses of the Bath.
33. Wives of Knights Commanders of the Bath.
34. Wives of Knights Bachelors.
35. Wives of the eldest Sons of the younger Sons of Peers.
36. Wives of the eldest Sons of Baronets.
37. Daughters of Baronets.
38. Wives of the eldest Sons of Knights of the Garter.
39. Wives of the eldest Sons of Bannerets.
40. Daughters of Bannerets.
41. Wives of the eldest Sons of Knights of the Bath.

42. Daughters of Knights of the Bath.

43. Wives of the eldest Sons of Knights Bachelors.

44. Daughters of Knights Bachelors.

45. Wives of the younger Sons of Baronets.

46. Daughters of Knights.

47. Wives of the Companions of the Order of the Bath.

48. Wives of the Esquires of the King's body.

49. Wives of the Esquires of the Knights of the Bath.

50. Wives of Esquires by creation.

51. Wives of Esquires by office.

52. Wives of the younger Sons of Knights of the Garter.

53. Wives of the younger Sons of Bannerets.

54. Wives of the younger Sons of Knights of the Bath.

55. Wives of the younger of Knights Bachelors.

56. Wives of Gentlemen entitled to bear arms.

57. Daughters of Esquires entitled to bear arms.

58. Daughters of Gentlemen entitled to bear arms.

59. Wives of Clergymen.

60. Wives of Barristers at Law.

61. Wives of Officers in the Navy.

62. Wives of Officers in the Army.

63. Wives of Citizens.

64. Wives of Burgesses.

65. Widows.

66. Daughters of Citizens.

67. Daughters of Burgesses.

N. B. Let those who have the priority of age be served first according to their precedency of title, but observe that age will not sanction you to serve a lady first who is in inferiority as to title, only on equal footing as to precedence; unless you should be otherwise ordered by your employers, &c. There is another kind of precedency, which is, being the wife of the greatest land-owner in a county; the lady who is wife to the greatest land-owner has the precedency at any public dinner given on any public occasion in the county. And supposing three sisters should be married to three lords, and the eldest sister's husband die; the younger sisters in this case must be served first: but if there should be any sisters not married, the widow should be served before the single ones; the same in every other class of precedency as in this: and likewise notice, that if there are young ladies in the family who invite company to dinner, &c. &c. those are served last, the strangers first. If you consider these observations, you will find the necessity of a servant having a personal knowledge of the ladies and gentlemen whom they may have to wait on, if they wish to wait properly and do things orderly. Some ladies and gentlemen, when carving, will say whom it is for; but if a strange servant be waiting, and does not know the names of the ladies and gentlemen, he is at a loss to know where to take it to; this is often the case; it is with myself when I go out to wait at large parties, and do not know the persons whom I have to wait on; therefore there is a necessity to employ our mind a little on this head, that we may wait properly; more particularly when serving the soup and fish round at dinner, and in taking up tea and refreshments into the drawing-room.

A Table of Precedency among Gentlemen, who ought to be served according to their respective Ranks.

1. King's Sons.
2. King's Brothers.
3. King's Uncles.
4. King's Grandsons.
5. King's Nephews.
6. Archbishop of Canterbury.
7. Lord High Chancellor.
8. Archbishop of York.
9. Lord Treasurer.
10. Lord President of the Privy Council.
11. Lord Privy Seal.
12. Lord High Constable.
13. Lord Great Chamberlain of England.
14. Earl Marshal.
15. Lord High Admiral.
16. Lord Steward of the Household.
17. Dukes according to their Patents.
18. Marquesses.
19. Duke's eldest Sons.
20. Earls.
21. Marquesses' eldest Sons.
22. Dukes' younger Sons.
23. Viscounts.
24. Earls' eldest Sons.
25. Marquesses' eldest Sons.
26. Bishop of London.
27. Bishop of Durham.
28. Bishop of Winchester.
29. Bishops according to their seniority of consecration.
30. Barons.
31. Speaker of the House of Commons.
32. Viscounts' eldest Sons.
33. Earls' younger Sons.
34. Barons' eldest Sons.
35. Knights of the Garter.
36. Privy Counsellors.
37. Chancellor of the Exchequer.
38. Chancellor of the Duchy of Lancaster.
39. Lord Chief Justice of the King's Bench.
40. The Master of the Rolls.
41. The Vice-Chancellor.
42. Lord Chief Justice of the Common Pleas.
43. Lord Chief Baron of the Exchequer.
44. Judges and Barons of the Exchequer according to seniority.
45. Knights Bannerets royal.
46. Viscounts' younger Sons.
47. Barons' younger Sons.
48. Baronets.
49. Knights Bannerets.
50. Knights of the Bath Grand Crosses.
51. Knights Commanders of the Bath.
52. Knights Bachelors.
53. Eldest Sons of the eldest Sons of Peers.

54. Baronets' eldest Sons.
55. Knights of the Garters' eldest Sons.
56. Bannerets' eldest Sons.
57. Knights of the Baths' eldest Sons.
58. Knights' eldest Sons.
59. Baronets' younger Sons.
60. Sergeants at Law.
61. Doctors, Deans, and Chancellors.
62. Masters in Chancery.
63. Companions of the Bath.
64. Esquires of the King's Body.
65. Gentlemen of the Privy Chamber.
66. Esquires of the Knights of the Bath.
67. Esquires by creation.
68. Esquires by office or commission.

69. Younger Sons of the Knights of the Garter.
70. Younger Sons of Bannerets.
71. Younger Sons of Knights of the Bath.
72. Younger Sons of Knights Bachelors.
73. Gentlemen entitled to bear arms.
74. Clergymen not dignitaries.
75. Barristers at Law.
76. Officers of the Navy.
77. Officers of the Army.
78. Citizens.
79. Burgesses.
80. Married Men and Widowers, before Single Men of the same rank.

There are many more degrees of precedency among the nobility and dignitaries of the Church according to their seniority, patents, and consecration, as you will find if you look over the Peerage and Baronetage, &c. &c.; this will show you the precedency under each head, also of the officers both in the army and navy, according to their degree of rank. Of those who are equal in point of precedency, let the eldest be served the first: this rule must be observed in all the classes.

Laws respecting Servants.

The following abstracts of Acts of Parliament respecting servants, ought to be read and attended to, not only by all persons in service, but by masters and mistresses also.

A servant setting fire carelessly to a house, is liable to pay, on the oath of one witness, a hundred pounds to the sufferer, or be committed to prison and hard labour for eighteen months. 14 *Geo.* 3. *c.* 48.

Where servants are hired by the year, they cannot be put away before the expiration of that term, without some reasonable cause, to be allowed by one magistrate; nor after the ending of the term, without a quarter's warning, given before witness. If a master discharge a servant otherwise, he is liable to a penalty of forty shillings. *5 Eliz. c. 4.*

If a servant refuse to serve his term, he may be committed till he give security to serve the time; or he may be sent to the house of correction, and punished there as a disorderly person. *5 Eliz. c. 4. 7 Jac. c. 4.*

A yearly servant is not to be discharged, by reason of sickness, or any other disability by the act of God; nor may his wages be abated. *Dalt. 129.*

All hiring, without stipulation of time, is, strictly speaking, hiring for a year, and the law so construes it. *2 Inst. 42.*

Both master and servant may, however, part by mutual consent. A master detaining a servant's wages, or not allowing sufficient meat, drink, &c. is a good cause for a servant's leaving his place; but it must be allowed by a justice of peace. *Dalt.*

If a servant hired for a term, quit his service before the end of it, he loses all his wages, unless his master puts him away.

A woman servant who marries, is obliged to serve out her time; and, if both man and wife are servants by the year, they must both serve their time. *Dalt. 92.*

Should a woman with child hire herself for a term, and the master she hires with knew not of her being with child, he may discharge her, but before a magistrate. If she prove with child during her service, he may do the same; but if he do not discharge her before a magistrate, when he knows of it, and keeps her on, he must provide for her till her delivery, and one month after, and then she is to be sent to her place of settlement. *Dalt.*

A servant hired at a month's wages, or warning, cannot quit his place, or be discharged a day before the expiration of the month, without the whole month's wages be paid; unless by the authority of a magistrate, for some reasonable complaint. If a servant, after warning given, is insolent, or refuses to do his duty, a magistrate, on complaint, will commit him to prison, for the time he has to serve; but the master will be ordered to pay him his wages whilst there.

No agreement a servant shall make with his master to his disadvantage, whilst he is under the age of 21, shall operate against him. *Dalt. c.* 58.

If a servant assault his master or mistress, or any other having charge over him, he may be bound over to his good behaviour, or be committed for a year, or less, at the discretion of two magistrates. 5 *Eliz. c.* 4. *s.* 21.

If any servant shall purloin, or make away with his master's goods, to the value of 40*s.* it is felony. 12 *Ann. c.* 7.

Disputes with servants about wages, under 10*l.* a year, and other things, if they cannot be amicably settled, should be referred to a neighbouring magistrate, who is authorized to hear complaints, and redress them; the expense is but trifling. But the wages of coachmen, grooms, and the like, magistrates can take no cognizance of.

If masters, or mistresses, when they hire servants, deliver into the custody of such servants, plate, china, linen, &c. and tell them, before witness, they must be responsible for such things; then, if they lose any part of them, the law will oblige them, as far as they are able, to replace them. As to breaking of china, a servant cannot be compelled to make it good, unless it was done designedly, and the servant, when hired, agreed to pay for what he broke.

A servant may stand up in his master's or mistress's defence, and assault any one that assaults them, without being liable to any punishment by law. 1 *Salk.* 407.

Whatever trespass a servant commits, by order of his master, the master is answerable for it, not the servant. *Lord Raymond*, 264.

Masters are justifiable in insisting on their servants going to church. Every person who shall keep a servant that shall be absent from church one month, without a reasonable excuse, shall forfeit 10*l.* for

3

every month he so keeps that servant. 3 *Jac. c.* 5. *s.* 8, 22.

Servants gaming at a public-house, with cards, dice, draughts, shuffle-board, Mississippi, skittles, nine-pins, billiard-tables, &c. are liable to be apprehended, and forfeit from 5*s.* to 20*s.* one fourth to the informer, or be committed to hard labour for a month, or till the penalty is paid. 30 *Geo.* 2. *c.* 24.

Masters are responsible for the acts of servants who act by their direction.

If any servant shall curse or swear, and be convicted, on the oath of one witness, before one justice, within eight days of the offence, he shall forfeit 1*s.* for the first offence, 2*s.* if convicted a second time, and 3*s.* the third time; or be committed to hard labour for ten days. 19 *Geo.* 2. *c.* 21.

Every person convicted of having been drunk, within six months of the complaint made, before one justice, on the oath of one witness, shall forfeit 5*s.* for the first offence, or be set in the stocks for six hours; and, if convicted a second time, shall give security not to offend so again. 4 *Jac. c.* 5. 21 *Jac. c.* 7.

If a master deliver the key of a room to a servant, and he steal to the value of one shilling, it is felony. *Dalt. c.* 155.

If any goods be delivered to the care of a servant, and he go away with them, or convert them to his own use, it is felony, if he be more than 18 years old. 21 *Hen.* 8. *c.* 7.

Servants pawning their masters' goods, without orders, shall forfeit 20*s.* and the value of the goods so pawned, or be sent to the house of correction for three months, and publicly whipped. 29 *Geo.* 3.

Such goods unlawfully pawned may be searched for, by a search-warrant, and shall be restored to the owner. *Ibid.*

A useful TABLE of EXPENSES, INCOME, or WAGES; showing, at one View, what any Sum, from One Pound to One Thousand per Annum, is per Calendar Month, Week, or Day.

Per Yr. *l.*	*s.*		Per Month. *l.*	*s.*	*d.*	Per Week. *l.*	*s.*	*d.*	Per Day. *l.*	*s.*	*d.*
1	0	is	0	1	8	0	0	4½	0	0	0¾
1	10	..	0	2	6	0	0	7	0	0	1
2	0	..	0	3	4	0	0	9¼	0	0	1¼
2	2	..	0	3	6	0	0	9¾	0	0	1½
2	10	..	0	4	2	0	0	11½	0	0	1¾
3	0	..	0	5	0	0	1	1¾	0	0	2
3	3	..	0	5	3	0	1	2½	0	0	2
3	10	..	0	5	10	0	1	4¼	0	0	2¼
4	0	..	0	6	8	0	1	6½	0	0	2¾
4	4	..	0	7	0	0	1	7½	0	0	2¾
4	10	..	0	7	6	0	1	8¾	0	0	3
5	0	..	0	8	4	0	1	11	0	0	3¼
5	5	..	0	8	9	0	2	0¼	0	0	3½
5	10	..	0	9	2	0	2	1½	0	0	3¾
6	0	..	0	10	0	0	2	3¾	0	0	4
6	6	..	0	10	6	0	2	5	0	0	4¼
6	10	..	0	10	10	0	2	6	0	0	4¼
7	0	..	0	11	8	0	2	8¼	0	0	4½
7	7	..	0	12	3	0	2	10	0	0	4¾
7	10	..	0	12	6	0	2	10½	0	0	5
8	0	..	0	13	4	0	3	1	0	0	5¼

Per Year. *l.*	*s.*		Per Mon. *l.*	*s.*	*d.*	Per Week. *l.*	*s.*	*d.*	Per Day. *l.*	*s.*	*d.*
8	8	is	0	14	0	0	3	2¾	0	0	5½
8	10	..	0	14	2	0	3	3¼	0	0	5½
9	0	..	0	15	0	0	3	5½	0	0	6
9	9	..	0	15	9	0	3	7½	0	0	6¼
10	0	..	0	16	8	0	3	10	0	0	6½
10	10	..	0	17	6	0	4	0½	0	0	7
11	0	..	0	18	4	0	4	3	0	0	7¼
11	11	..	0	19	3	0	4	5¼	0	0	7½
12	0	..	1	0	0	0	4	7½	0	0	8
12	12	..	1	1	0	0	4	10	0	0	8¼
13	0	..	1	1	8	0	5	0	0	0	8½
13	13	..	1	2	9	0	5	3	0	0	9
14	0	..	1	3	4	0	5	4½	0	0	9¼
14	14	..	1	4	6	0	5	8	0	0	9¾
15	0	..	1	5	0	0	5	9	0	0	10
15	15	..	1	6	3	0	6	0½	0	0	10¼
16	0	..	1	6	8	0	6	2	0	0	10½
16	16	..	1	8	0	0	6	5½	0	0	11
17	0	..	1	8	4	0	6	6½	0	0	11¼
17	17	..	1	9	9	0	6	10½	0	0	11¾
18	0	..	1	10	0	0	6	11	0	0	11¾

Per Year. *l.*	*s.*		Per Month. *l.*	*s.*	*d.*	Per Week. *l.*	*s.*	*d.*	Per Day. *l.*	*s.*	*d.*
18	18	is	1	11	6	0	7	3	0	1	0½
19	0	..	1	11	8	0	7	3½	0	1	0½
20	0	..	1	13	4	0	7	8	0	1	1¼
30	0	..	2	10	0	0	11	6	0	1	7¾
40	0	..	3	6	8	0	15	4½	0	2	2¼
50	0	..	4	3	4	0	19	3	0	2	9
60	0	..	5	0	0	1	3	0¾	0	3	3½
70	0	..	5	16	8	1	6	11	0	3	10
80	0	..	6	13	4	1	10	9	0	4	4½
90	0	..	7	10	0	1	14	7¼	0	4	11
100	0	..	8	6	8	1	18	5½	0	5	5¾
200	0	..	16	13	4	3	16	11	0	10	11½
300	0	..	25	0	0	5	15	4½	0	16	5¼
400	0	..	33	6	8	7	13	10	1	1	11
500	0	..	41	13	4	9	12	3½	1	7	4¾
600	0	..	50	0	0	11	10	9	1	12	10½
700	0	..	58	6	8	13	9	2¾	1	18	4¼
800	0	..	66	13	4	15	7	8¼	2	3	10
900	0	..	75	0	0	17	6	1¾	2	9	3¾
1000	0	..	83	6	8	19	4	7¼	2	14	9½

CALCULATION OF POSTING,

From One Shilling to Two Shillings and Sixpence per Mile.

	12d.	13d.	14d.	15d.	16d.	17d.	18d.	2s.	2s. 6d.
	s. d.	s. d.	s. d.	s. d.	s. d.	s. d.	s. d.	s. d.	s. d.
Eight Miles	8 0	8 8	9 4	10 0	10 8	11 4	12 0	16 0	20 0
Nine	9 0	9 9	10 6	11 3	12 0	12 9	13 6	18 0	22 6
Ten	10 0	10 10	11 8	12 6	13 4	14 2	15 0	20 0	25 0
Eleven	11 0	11 11	12 10	13 9	14 8	15 7	16 6	22 0	27 6
Twelve	12 0	13 0	14 0	15 0	16 0	17 0	18 0	24 0	30 0
Thirteen	13 0	14 1	15 2	16 3	17 4	18 5	19 6	26 0	32 6
Fourteen	14 0	15 2	16 4	17 6	18 8	19 10	21 0	28 0	35 0
Fifteen	15 0	16 3	17 6	18 9	20 0	21 3	22 6	30 0	37 6
Sixteen	16 0	17 4	18 8	20 0	21 4	22 8	24 0	32 0	40 0
Seventeen	17 0	18 5	19 10	21 3	22 8	24 1	25 6	34 0	42 6
Eighteen	18 0	19 6	21 0	22 6	24 0	25 6	27 0	36 0	45 0
Nineteen	19 0	20 7	22 2	23 9	25 4	26 11	28 6	38 0	47 6
Twenty	20 0	21 8	23 4	25 0	26 8	28 4	30 0	40 0	50 0

THE END.

Printed by S. Gosnell, Little Queen Street, London.

OTHER TITLES AVAILABLE FROM PRYOR PUBLICATIONS

Don't
A Manual of Mistakes & Improprieties more or less prevalent in Conduct and Speech

A best seller in the 1880s and once again in our facsimile edition (over 100,000 copies sold) *Don't* is a reflection of a society long since past. It makes for fascinating and amusing reading now.

Don't trouble people with your domestic mishaps, with accounts of your rebellious servants, or with complaints of any kind.
Don't neglect to keep to the right of the promenade, otherwise there may be collisions and much confusion.
Don't wear diamonds in the morning.

Originally published 1880. Size 13cm x 10cm

112 Pages. ISBN 0 946014 02 7 £4.⁰⁰

EVERYBODY'S BOOK OF CORRECT CONDUCT
Being The Etiquette Of Everyday Life

'It is certain that he who lives correctly every day will find himself following the higher laws of morality and rectitude.' So says the Preface to this book that has contents ranging from The Duties of Life and The Pleasures of Life to The Formation of Habit; The Heart and Conscience, Conversation and Out-of-Door Life.

Originally published 1893. Size 13cm x 10.5cm

192 Pages Paperback. ISBN 0 946014 37 X £4.⁹⁹

MANNERS FOR MEN

Mrs. Humphry, who is also the author of *Manners for Women,*
wrote 'Like every other woman I have my ideal of manhood. The
difficulty is to describe it. First of all, he must be a gentleman, but
that means so much that it, in its turn, requires explanation . . .'

First published 1897   176 pages   Size: 20cm x 10cm
ISBN: 0 946014 23 X   Paperback   **£4.**⁵⁰

MANNERS FOR WOMEN

Can anything be nicer than a really nice girl? 'may seem quaint
but it is a useful reminder that tittering is an unpleasant habit
and curtseying should be avoided unless you know what you are
doing.' *The Times.*

First published 1897   164 pages   Size: 20cm x 10cm
ISBN: 0 946014 17 5   Paperback   **£4.**⁵⁰

THE NATURAL HISTORY OF STUCK-UP PEOPLE

ALBERT SMITH

'We are about to expose, as simply and truthfully as we can,
the foolish conventionalities of a large proportion of the middle classes of the present day, who believe that position is
attained by climbing up a staircase of moneybags.'
Delightfully illustrated.

Originally published 1847   128 pages   Size: 13cm x 10.5cm
ISBN: 0 946014 39 6   Paperback   Illustrated   **£4.**⁰⁰

Albert Smith was one of the greatest showmen of the 19th century. His enter-
tainments were as popular a feature of the capital as Madame Tussaud's and
the Tower of London. This book was one of a series of fictionalised accounts
that were very popular with Victorian readers.

EVERYBODY'S BOOK OF EPITAPHS

Being For The Most Part What The Living Think Of The Dead

Here lies my wife, a sad slattern and shrew
If I said I regretted her, I should lie too!

A look at epitaphs for the famous to the poor - some amusing,
some sad, some historic, some enlightening, all fascinating.

Here lies John Wherdle, Parish Beedle
Who was so very knowing
His wisdom's gone, and so is he,
Because he left off growing.

Originally published 1885   Size: 13.5cm x 10.5cm
ISBN: 0 946014 38 8   128 pages   Paperback   **£4.**⁵⁰

A full list of our publications sent on request. All books post and packing free in the U.K.

PRYOR PUBLICATIONS

75 Dargate Road, Yorkletts, Whitstable, Kent CT5 3AE.

Tel/Fax: (01227) 274655